faith and little children

Karen Leslie

faith and little children

A Guide for Parents and Teachers

TWENTY-THIRD PUBLICATIONS
Mystic, Connecticut

Twenty-Third Publications
185 Willow Street
P.O. Box 180
Mystic, CT 06355
(203) 536-2611

© 1990 Karen Leslie. All rights reserved. No part of this publication my be reproduced in any manner without prior written permission for the publisher. Write to Permissions Editor.

ISBN 0-89622-404-x
Library of Congress Catalog Card No. 89-51903

Contents

CHAPTER 1
Religious Education for Preschool and Kindergarten 1

CHAPTER 2
God, Jesus and the Bible 5

CHAPTER 3
The Team: Parents and Teachers 9
    Parents 10
    Teachers 14

CHAPTER 4
Teaching about the Church 19
    Church Family 22
    Baptism 28
    The Mass 33
    The Church Building 39

CHAPTER 5
Celebrating the Liturgical Year 42
    Celebrating Advent 45
    Celebrating Christmas 52
    Celebrating Valentine's Day 58
    Celebrating Lent 64
    Celebrating Easter 72
    Celebrating Pentecost 80
    Celebrating Mary 84
    Celebrating Saints 90
    Celebrating Thanksgiving 97

Appendix 104
    Prayer Services for Young Children 105
    Paraphrased Bible Verses 107
    Audiovisual Resources 108
    Publishers' Addresses 112

CHAPTER 1

Religious Education for Preschool and Kindergarten

It is always very interesting to gather reactions from people when you tell them you teach a religious education class for three-, four-, or five-year-olds. "What can you possibly teach them? Do they really understand religion? Aren't you going to teach them the Our Father? When are you going to tell them about the sacraments? Why are you talking about flowers and animals?" As religious educators of little ones, we need to realize that our programs are "religion readiness" programs. Our purpose is to begin to build a foundation of experiences that future catechists will build upon. Remember what Jesus said about a house built upon a foundation of rock? We in preschool or kindergarten religious education are providing the groundwork for further catechetical instruction. How do we accomplish such a task?

It is always a good idea to begin at the beginning! And so

our first task is to realize just how little ones learn. Children think differently than adults do, and at this early stage in their lives they are only able to deal in the concrete, sensual world. That is, they can assimilate and learn only through their senses; through what they can see, hear, touch, taste and feel. They are not psychologically or mentally ready for the abstract, for signs or symbols. That is why a good preschool/kindergarten program will focus on what the children are most familiar with: family, friends, animals, trees, all of creation. Children need to know God *first* as Father and Creator of all the good gifts they have. They need to be encouraged to find God in the wonders around them and to realize that God is part of all life. (And not just present for one hour on a Sunday morning!)

As an example of how the little ones learn, consider the topic of water. As we present the lesson, we concentrate on the many things water does: it washes and cleanses, all things need it to live and grow, we play in it, it quenches our thirst, etc. The children learn about water in a manner they can understand. They are made to realize that water is a gift God gives us because he loves us so much. Later, as they learn about baptism and hear Jesus call himself the "living water," they can draw upon what they have experienced in their early years. A three- to five-year-old child cannot possibly understand at this point in their development what Jesus means by calling himself the "living water," but *can* understand how good a glass of water tastes on a very hot day. We need to be where the children "are" and not try to rush or confuse their understanding. We need to think as children, see as children, become children!

Little ones form their concept of God by dealing with all the people and things around them. Their sense of wonder and awe must be stimulated and directed to the source, the creator of all the good things that surround them. The more varied the experiences we offer the children, the more diverse their concept of God will be. They will discover God involved in all areas of their lives. They may not find the words to describe their idea of God, but God will speak and be revealed to them in ways they can understand. We need to work with God and expose the wonders of creation to the children. And not only do we want to "expose" the children to the wonders around them; we also need to get excited about them ourselves! Children always learn more by what we do than by what we say, and if our reaction to the sunset, the flower or the spider's web is mediocre, they are able to sense that lack of excitement.

Our attitude is actually more important than the lesson we present, as it impacts one very important objective we have in preschool religious education, that of proper attitude development in the children. We are not so much trying to "teach" our little ones facts; we are endeavoring to develop in them an attitude of belonging to our church family. Our classes are their "church," the place where they find friends, loving acceptance, and happiness. Our classes are places where the children are able to celebrate God's love and care at a level and in a manner which they can understand. Preschool and kindergarten classes are the three- to five-year-olds' "little church," their own liturgy, so to speak. It is a well-known fact that attitudes are learned very early in life and the importance of developing an attitude of belonging in our church family at an early age cannot be underestimated. Remember how Jesus treated the little children who came to him? He welcomed them and blessed them. He did not sit them down and "teach" them. We need to do as Jesus did: to welcome and bless our little ones, to accept and love them. The best indicator of our success as preschool catechists is whether the children like to come to class. If they do, we have succeeded in making them feel a part of our church family; we have blessed them as Jesus did.

There is another extremely important objective of preschool religious education and that deals with the religious development of the parents. This topic will be dealt with in Chapter 3, The Team: Parents and Teachers. At this point, suffice it to say that it's not only the children we are teaching!

As preschool and kindergarten catechists, we are foundation builders, we are seed planters. We don't always get to see the completed building or the flowering plant, for someone else usually finishes the job. Without our initial endeavors, however, no growth will occur. We are the vital first step in the children's journey of faith.

CHAPTER 2

God, Jesus and the Bible

How do we begin to "teach" little ones about God, to instill in them a sense of awe, wonder and love for the almighty source of all life and being? At the beginning, of course! Our first experience of God is through the marvels he has created. From our very first moments of life, we begin to enjoy the lavish gifts of the Creator: our parents' love, food, warmth, clothes, home, all the gifts our senses can assimilate. We learn to know and love God through the works he performs and the wonderful gifts he has bestowed on us; being human and "sensual" (experiencing through the senses), there is no other way!

In our preschool/kindergarten religious education classes, we need to introduce the children to God the Creator, our Father, by making them aware of all the wonders that surround them. This is the concept of God that the children will be most able to identify with: a loving Father, a giver of gifts. In all that we speak about and present in our classes, we need to remind the children that everything is a gift from God, given because God loves us so much.

We also want to speak to our little ones about Jesus, the very special gift that God the Father sent us. Christmas provides an especially appropriate time to introduce Jesus to the children as we relate the story of his birth. It is very important to remember to always talk about Jesus in very human terms, emphasizing his goodness and kindness. For our preschoolers, his purpose for living on earth was to show us how God wants us to live and to treat other people. The children are not able to understand his role as redeemer and savior and presentation of the crucifixion and resurrection stories are not appropriate at this age.

I remember a visit our pastor made to our five-year-old class during Lent. He asked the children if they knew what happened on Good Friday. One little boy (obviously schooled by his parents as we don't teach "Good Friday" in our early childhood program) answered, "Jesus died on the cross." Pleased at his answer, the pastor proceeded to ask him what happened on Easter Sunday. (I knew Father was pushing his luck!) The little boy said, "Jesus rose from the dead," and knowingly added, "and he came back as a ghost to get those bad men who did that to him!" I think the pastor left the classsroom finally realizing why we don't teach these concepts at this age! The religious truths, knowledge of the political situation at the time, and the faith response required to study this saving event is far beyond the comprehension of three-, four-, and five-year-olds.

The stories of Jesus' miracles should also be reserved for later instruction. The children may regard these miracles as mere magic or as tricks they see on television and may dismiss them as unreal. Whenever Jesus performed a miracle, he called for a faith reponse or had already witnessed a proclamation of faith (i.e., the woman caught in adultery and the centurion). This profession of faith that accompanies the miracle stories cannot be understood by our little ones. The children may also take these stories quite literally and pray for and expect a "healing," and be very confused and angry upon the death of a pet or a beloved grandparent.

From the discussion above, we realize that we must be very careful in presenting stories from the life of Jesus. It is best to concentrate on stories that emphasize the kindness, caring and love of Jesus for other people. We must make the life of Jesus real for our little ones by making them realize that they, too, can be like him in being kind, loving, and helpful. This is the way they will be able to understand Jesus and to follow him at their young age.

The Bible is a book that relates the story of God's relationship with his people. It is also an "adult" book and needs to be read prayerfully and with some understanding of the literary genres it uses. Reading the Bible to little ones or using Bible stories (especially those in the Old Testament) should be discouraged. Our preschool/kindergarten children should be taught that the Bible is a very special book that tells us stories about God and Jesus. Most verses and stories that we would choose to use should be paraphrased so that the little ones can understand them.

There are wonderful ways to retell these favorite Bible stories. Some examples of this technique can be found in Chapter 5, in the sections presenting Lent ("Jesus and the Children" and "The Loaves and Fishes") and Valentine's Day ("The Good Samaritan"). By paraphrasing a Bible story in this manner, the children will be able to understand the concept that is being presented. We need to present the story in terms and in a situation that the children may have experienced and will understand. There are several stories that can be presented in this manner, but for the most part, Bible stories should be reserved for presentation when the children are older. Bible verses are easily used in very simple prayer services or litany-type prayers, but may also have to be paraphrased or simplified somewhat.

Parents and pastors may try to pressure you into teaching more "religious" topics: memorized prayers, Bible stories, devotional practices, etc. (We honestly had a parent ask us one time when we were going to teach the sacraments!) But remember what you are about in early childhood religious education! We are not interested in teaching the children facts and stories that they can rattle off like television commercial jingles with no understanding of what they are saying. Our main purpose is to develop their sense of awe and wonder and to instill a sense of thanksgiving in our children as we introduce them to the Father, our Creator, and his Son, Jesus. And we do this in a manner and with methods that are appropriate and understandable to their young age. This formidable task is a "team" effort and requires the cooperation of both catechists (teachers) and parents to bring the children to a sense of their God.

CHAPTER 3

The Team: Parents and Teachers

Although *Sharing the Light of Faith*, the National Catechetical Directory for Catholics of the United States, is not on the "best seller" list, it is a very important and timely document. Prepared by the bishops of the United States, this volume organizes principles and guidelines for catechesis (doctrinal instruction) in the United States. There is an interesting statement in section 230 regarding the catechesis of preschool children: "Preschool programs should focus mainly on parents, providing them with opportunities to deepen their faith and become more adept at helping their children form a foundation of that life of faith which will gradually develop and manifest itself." Catechists of preschool children may think, "Great, so how am I supposed to do that? I thought we were into flowers, birds, friends, and animals. How am I supposed to instruct parents, too?"

The key word in the bishops' statement is *opportunities;* we need to provide parents with opportunities to deepen their faith. And there are several ways that we can accomplish this as preschool and kindergarten religious educators.

PARENTS

The ideal way to begin to accomplish this goal is to meet with the parents directly. Some programs have instructional or informational gatherings for parents at the same time the children are in class. This is truly a utopian situation, however, and most programs find that with the children's classes usually held at the same time as liturgy, weekly parent meetings are not feasable. However, several parent meetings during the course of the year should be within reach of most programs and are indeed imperative to the success of the program. When, how, and what are some questions you may be asking yourself about these meetings. The following sections will provide some information to answer your questions and allay some of your fears.

There should always be a meeting with parents at the beginning of the school year. It is absolutely necessary that parents understand the philosophy and objectives (see Chapter 1) of your program in order to gain their support and cooperation. This would also be a good time to introduce or reinforce the concept that parents are the main religious educators of their children. This is a difficult idea for some parents to handle, as many of them feel that if their children are enrolled in a church-school program, that's all there is to it; they've met their responsibility. Many parents feel that they are not "qualified" to teach their children about their faith and want to leave it to the "professionals." As catechists, we need to encourage parents and to provide them with information, events, and experiences that will better enable them to pass their faith to their children.

Some thoughts that you could use to present these concepts to parents at an initial meeting are given here.

If there is one concept that would be chosen as the most important thing you need to know about your children's religious education, it is this: *You* are the main religious educators of your children. The job does not belong solely to the priest, the sister, the Religious Ed program, or the Catholic school. The main responsibility belongs to you, the parents. You must realize that at this point, we only have your children for one hour a week; they are with you the rest of the time. Your family relationships and the way you act toward each other provide the very foundation for your children's faith development. Many of us were not brought up this way or trained to think this way. "Holy Mother Church" was precisely that; a mother who told us what to do. Vatican Council II has changed that perspective; we are called to be adult members of our faith community. We are to be responsible for developing our own faith lives and to be examples to our children with the guidance of the church. There are several ways to be effective religious educators of your children.

The first thing you must do is to love your children. This sounds easy enough to do! However, this love entails making your children feel secure and accepted, to build your children's self-esteem. This is not always an easy task. Remember, there are no bad children; only children who do bad things. You need to tell your children that you love them. Hug them and hold them, read to them and play with them. And dads, don't think that this "religion thing" is just for mom. The first way that children learn about God is that God is our father. If children do not have a good image about

"Dad," their image of God the Father will suffer. So, dads, your role is important!

Loving your children also entails discipline; that is, setting limits and guidelines and correcting when errors are made. A story was once told about a family who had a large beautiful backyard at their house. The only problem was that the backyard was edged with high drop-offs. The little girl in the family was afraid to play in the backyard; she was afraid to run or venture very far from the house because she had been warned about the drop-offs. Then her family installed a fence all around the backyard (they set a limit). After that, the little girl felt free enough to run and play and use the entire backyard. The fence had actually provided her some freedom. This is what your discipline should do for your children; provide them with the freedom to develop into the best people they can be.

The second thing you need to do to be an effective religious educator of your children is to develop your own faith life. Remember, you can't give what you don't have. You cannot force children to believe what you do. You need to live what you believe, and pray and hope that they catch it. Faith is caught, not taught! If you are a little uncomfortable with that or feel that you have been neglectful of your faith life, begin to reinvestigate your faith. Start really paying attention to the Sunday homilies and make them part of your life. Begin to read Scripture, subscribe to some Catholic publications, take an adult education course, join a faith sharing group, etc. The development of your faith is a lifetime process, so if you've "taken a break," it's time to set out on the journey again.

As you build and live your own faith, it is important that you develop a sense of God for yourself, a personal relationship and friendship with God. As you do this, you will be able to share God with your children, which is the third way to be an effective religious educator. Make God present to them in all that they do and see. Look for "teachable moments" with your children; go for a walk and thank God for all the gifts in nature, pray at meals and before bed, thank God for all the good things God has given and done for you, etc. Your actions and attitudes will be the ways your children will gain a sense of God and finally a commitment to a Christian way of life. Your children need to see you pray, to go to church, to treat others kindly, etc. This is the way you will most effectively educate your children in the faith.

While this first meeting with parents is most important, continuing communication with them will make their job as the main religious educators of their children easier. There are several ways you can do this. You can schedule several other informational meetings, selecting topics that are of interest to your parents. You can also schedule sessions which both the adults and children attend together. These could be done in conjunction with the holidays, planning a filmstrip or story, a craft, some songs and a snack that parents and children could enjoy together.

Another very effective way of communicating with your parents is by making sure that some type of take-home material goes home each week with the children explaining the theme of the lesson and possibly activities that the parents can do with their children to reinforce the lesson. (Many preschool and kindergarten programs include this type of material.) Try to include some special activities, such as Advent calendars, instructions for an Advent wreath, etc. In this way you are providing the parents with material that they can use in their home to further the religious education of their child.

TEACHERS

In Chapter 1, the preschool and kindergarten religious education class was called the children's "little church," their own "liturgy" so to speak. It is important for the catechist (or teacher) to understand this comparison herself as well as be able to explain it to the parents. The following is an examination of a sample division of class time and activities and how it relates to our liturgy.

The first event in the classroom is to gather the children together. Many teachers do this with a song or a prayer. Another good way to do this is to have a very simple procession and Bible enthronement ceremony with the children. These methods of gathering the children easily relate to the entrance procession, the gathering hymn, and the greetings exchanged between the celebrant and the congregation. Usually the lesson or theme of the day is presented next, utilizing some storytelling technique. Our lessons are presented to us through the reading of holy Scripture at Mass. After the story is presented to the children, there is usually a time for talking and listening about the story, just as the homily provides us with an opportunity to listen to the explanation of the readings. The snack that the children share is of course related to the eucharist and we pray with the children at various times during the class just as we pray at Mass. The craft provides the children with an "experience" of the lesson just as we must go out and live our lessons. And we naturally close the class with wishes for a good week (or a blessing) and possibly a song.

All of these "liturgical" elements of our class with the little ones are preparing them for an appreciation of the liturgy at a later age. With an understanding of these elements, parents and catechists alike are mindful of the fact that our classes are not just a babysitting service. They are the places where the children celebrate God's love and their little Christian community in a manner they can understand and appreciate. With this understanding of what our classes and programs are all about, it will be evident that parents and catechists are *partners* in the faith development of the children.

In presenting this "little liturgy," there are certain basic activities and techniques used that are adapted to suit the three-, four-, and five-year-olds.

To begin class and gather the children, a Bible enthronement or prayer service can effectively be used. A very simple format for these services will suffice for the little ones. First, be sure to have a prayer corner or area set up. This can be done very easily with a tablecloth or cloth napkin, a candle, a plant, or artificial flowers, and the Bible. You may also have objects on your prayer table that relate to the lesson, ie., a colored leaf for fall, a mirror for "I am special," an apple for fruits, a stuffed lamb for Easter, etc. Begin with a procession from the back of your classroom while singing a very simple song. The "Alleluia Round" by Carey Landry (from the album *Bloom Where You're Planted*) is an excellent processional song or you can compose your own using familiar childhood tunes. Allow the children to carry the items from your prayer table in the procession (it is best not to light the candle) and place them on the table. Gather the children around the table and say a brief opening prayer that relates to the theme of your class for the day. Take the Bible from the table and read (paraphrase if necessary) a verse or an appropriate story. Be sure to say to the children, "Our Bible says," or "This is a story from our Bible." Say a short litany prayer with the children, having them answer very simply, "Thank you, God," or "We love you, God." Close the service with the same song that was used for the procession or choose another. Of course, any of these suggested parts can be altered or eliminated to suit your class.

After greeting the children warmly, you will want to present your lesson for the day. One of the best ways to do this is by using a story. Jesus often chose to use stories to illustrate his lesson, and the little ones love to listen to stories. One important thing to remember is that the children will remember more of what they *see* than of what they merely hear, so it is important to use good visual aids when you tell your story. Use a book containing large pictures, or use a flannel board with figures that are purchased or home made. (Figures can easily be made using coloring books or magazine pictures and gluing a piece of flannel or felt to the back so that they will stick to the flannel board.) You can also use puppets, purchased or homemade (from paper bags, paper plates and popsicle sticks, socks, etc.) or use articles from the story that you are telling. For example, if you are telling a story about planting seeds, bring a small trowel, some seeds, a watering can, etc. It is also important to *tell* the story, not read it. Know your story well enough that you'll be able to tell it easily; you may have to practice! After you tell the story, you may want to have the children tell the story to you, using the visual aids that you employed. This is a very good way to reinforce the lesson.

Three-, four-, and five-year-olds have a short attention span (about 7-10 minutes) so it is always a good idea to alternate active and quiet activities. After you present your lesson, the children will need to move about. Use songs or fingerplays for this purpose. There are many books listing such resources in the library or from teachers' book clubs. There are some very nice songbooks available from Warren Publishing House for young children. All the songs in these books are "piggyback songs," or songs that have been written to the tunes of familiar childhood songs, so you don't need any musical ability to use the books. (Write to Warren Publishing House, P.O. Box 2255, Everett, WA 98203 for ordering information and for a catalogue of all their early childhood resources.) You can also use some very simple exercises or games with the children to "get them moving."

Snack time is a very important part of the class, yet should be kept simple. Snacks that the children can share, such as fruit or a loaf of bread are meaningful expressions of "breaking bread together." Having children pass out the snack that they have brought to class also teaches the children to share and to say "thank you" as it is handed to them. If your facilities permit, it is sometimes fun to allow the children to make their own snack for the day. Instant pudding, popcorn, peanut butter crackers, or sandwiches, baked refrigerated biscuit shapes are just a few ideas that will work well.

As was stated, children remember more of what they see than of what they hear. They remember the *most* of what they *do*, and that is why a craft project is so important in the early childhood class. It should involve the largest slot of time in your lesson plan. It is important to remember that your craft should be one that the children can do themselves, with little adult assistance.

Our objective in having the children do a project is to make them feel good about themselves and their achievements and this will not be accomplished if the teacher or helper does most of the craft. We are not making craft projects for the *parents*, so don't worry if the finished project is not perfect!

The closing of your class can very simply be wishes for a good week, a song, prayer, or blessing. You can extend your hands over the children and say a short prayer for them or you could sign their forehead with the sign of the cross as they leave. Explain to them what you are doing; the cross is the sign of how much God loves us. Stand and extend your arms out at your sides at shoulder level. Tell the children that God loves them this much (as wide as your arms are extended), and show them that your body forms a cross. That's why you will make the sign of the cross on their forehead.

Don't ever be concerned if something in your class is not "working right." There are some days when even the quietest class creates mayhem! Make sure that you always try to fit your lesson plan to the children, not the children to your plan. Always have "plan B" ready, which may simply be some extra story books or a list of songs, games, or fingerplays that you can use.

The most important thing about your class is not how involved or impressive your lesson plan is or how many things the children can "rattle off," but how much they enjoy coming each week. This is not to say that there is no need to plan and that you can just "wing it." But the most important thing that you want to accomplish in your class is an attitude of belonging to their church family. If the children are anxious to attend, enjoy being there, and are finding loving acceptance and care, then you may consider your class a success.

Go and plan your lessons in peace!

CHAPTER 4

Teaching about the Church

If you ask the average Catholic for a definition of the church, you would get as many different answers as the number of people you ask. You would receive the "legal" definitions, the "spiritual" definitions and all sorts of explanations that would fall in-between. When speaking of the church to the young child, we must compare and relate it to something with which they are already familiar. The obvious comparison in this case is to compare the church to the family unit, a concept with which all the children are familiar.

The importance of the family to the child's understanding of the church community cannot be overestimated. The family is in fact the children's first "church," the place where they find love, acceptance, and care for the special person that they are. In this era in which we are experiencing some breakdown in family communication and caring, it becomes more difficult to speak of a loving, caring family in some situations. It is imperative then to relate to the children the importance of values such as love, caring, helping, and sharing within a family unit and also among friends. In the classroom, the catechist will first want to present lessons on the family and the special place that the child has in that family and also a lesson on friends. (Ideas to accomplish this task will be provided in the discussion on Church Family which follows.) In the family itself, the importance of living the values one wants children to learn is the most basic and probably the only truly effective way to "pass on" the faith and the fact of membership in a church family. (Further discussion on this topic is found in Chapter 3.)

Once the children have been exposed to and have a basic idea of what a family is and how special their friends are, we are still confronted with the problem of defining the Church in a manner that the children can understand. A very basic definition that can be used with the children is the following: "The church family is a group of people who believe in Jesus and try to live the way he did by helping other people and showing love." The church family can be compared to the child's family in that all members of the family love each other and care about each other. They help each other and work together. They also celebrate and have fun together. It is extremely important that the children are taught at this very young age that the church is made up of people and that they themselves are part of the church family. By developing this attitude of belonging, we are laying the foundation for the children to assume "ownership" of the church and increasing the possibility of their active involvement in the community at a later time.

A child will discover a happy and secure "church" by being enrolled in some type of weekly religious education preschool or kindergarten class. In fact, this class becomes the child's "little church" because lessons are presented in a manner that the children can understand. It is difficult to assess the importance of having preschool and kindergarten children attend Mass each week. No child at this age will understand the liturgy; many become distracted (and distracting!) because of their inability to participate. Young children should certainly be taken to Mass occasionally, so that they are familiar with how the church family celebrates; holidays are very good times to do this. However, the young child will find more that he can understand and relate to in a preschool/kindergarten religious education class than he will at Mass at this point in his young life. The decision regarding how often the youngster will attend Mass certainly lies with the parents and no answer is appropriate for all children as they are so different. But attendance in a class designed specifically for their age group is highly recommended!

There are three lessons that are easily presented to the preschool and kindergarten child that will introduce them to the church in a manner that they will understand and enjoy. These are a lesson on 1) the church family, 2) baptism and 3) the Mass. Following are some ideas for presentation of such lessons in a class and also ideas that can be used at home. Please remember, however, that lessons on families and friends should proceed lessons on the church. It would also be very helpful if these lessons were presented after Christmas, after the children have been "introduced" to Jesus. In this way, we are able to build upon concepts and ideas in a progressive way.

After the lesson suggestions, there will be a section describing how to introduce the young child to the church building itself. Ideas for a "tour" will also be included.

There is one other important concept to remember in teaching young children about the church. The family and the classroom are places where they will learn about the love, care, affection and concern that are the hallmarks of our faith. It is this attitude and "living out" of the faith that will teach children the most. And this is perhaps the most difficult part of the job! Be sure to treat the children in a manner that "speaks" eloquently of your membership in the church. "See how they love one another!"

CHURCH FAMILY

"Whoever does the will of my heavenly Father is brother and sister and mother to me."   Matthew 12:50

The church as people, as a community of believers in Jesus Christ and his way of life, is an important concept for all Catholics to grasp. The main concern of church members is to help each other on the journey to the Father and to create in the community an attitude of love, sharing and concern that will attract others to a belief in Jesus. This concept is a fairly easy one for young children to grasp, as they are most familiar with the idea of family and are usually quite eager to discuss their parents, brothers, and sisters with you. They are also old enough to realize that Jesus is the person that we in the church family follow and that we want to act just like he did. (See the lesson presentation of "Lent" in Chapter 5 for a more detailed discussion of this topic.)

A good way to begin a discussion on families is with a book or a story about a family. There are many excellent books about families in the library or storybooks to purchase in grocery and drug stores. You may also use flannel board figures from a coloring book or catalog and talk about families. You will want to discuss all the special things a family is and does together. Families work together and help each other. They play together and have fun together. People in a family love each other and want to be with each other. Talk to the children about how their families work and play together and show love for each other. Perhaps you will want to use the following song and play as a circle game to reinforce your lesson.

(Tune: The Farmer in the Dell)
The family in our home, the family in our home,
Hi ho the derry-o, the family in our home.
The dad picks the mom, the dad picks the mom, etc.
The mom picks the brother,
The brother picks the sister,
The sister picks the dog,
We all work together,
We all love each other.

You may add your own verses to this song as you wish; it's a very versatile song!

Tell the children that our church family is very much like their own families. People in our church family want to do good things like God wants them to do. All the people help each other and want to be together. There are lots of families in our church family. Remind the children that all of their classmates are also in their church family.

The most important idea that we want the children to grasp is that the church is the people in our community and not just the building or the priest. Of course, we want the children to know who the pastor, or the "father" of the church family is. In fact, a visit to your class by the pastor would be ideal! If, however, we can begin to make the children, at this young age, realize that they are the church, we will develop an attitude of belonging that will stay with them throughout the development of their faith lives.

You can use the traditional fingerplay, "Here is the church, here is the steeple," for this part of the lesson. You may also want to change the words to the above song to fit the idea of church family. For example:

> The people in our church, the people in our church,
> Hi ho the derry-o, the people in our church.
> Regina picks Bobby, Regina picks Bobby, etc.
> Tommy picks Matthew *(use names of class members)*
> End: reform the circle and sing:
> We are all the church, we are all the church,
> We are all one family, we are all the church.

Or try the following song:
(Tune: London Bridges)
1. The church is people, we are one, we are one, we are one
   The church is people, we are one, clap your hands!
2. We help each other, etc.
3. We love each other, etc.
4. We sing together, etc.
5. We pray together, etc.
6. We live like Jesus, etc.

In your lesson on church family, talk to the children about the different "helpers" that are part of our church family. Just as everyone in our regular families needs to help each other and so have jobs to do, all the members of our church family have different jobs. Listed below are some "jobs" that people in the church family do and ways that you can explain their work to the children. The explanation will be more meaningful if you can use pictures or flannel board figures of the people or some of the objects these people would use.

1. Priest The priest is like the head of the family. He leads the church family when we get together to celebrate at Mass. He helps people get married, welcomes new babies into the church family by baptizing them, visits sick people in the hospital, and teaches us about God. The priest does lots of other things too; he is very busy all day helping the church family. (Make sure the children know the name(s) of your parish priest(s).

2. Sisters Sisters are ladies who are helpers in our church. They live with other sisters in a house called a convent. They pray together, eat together, and have many different jobs. Some are teachers, some are nurses, some work in church offices, and some work with poor people.

3. Lector This person reads the stories from the Bible at Mass. He helps our church family celebrate together.

4. Altar Boy This person helps the priest at Mass by holding the book for the priest to read from and getting things when the priest needs them.

5. Organist and Choir These people help us to sing at church. We are very happy when we can sing beautiful songs together!

6. Food Bank Helpers These people collect extra food and give it to people who don't have enough to eat.

Of course, you may add to this list or descriptions as you like. And don't forget to talk about yourself—you're a church helper, too!

Explain to the children that the church family also prays together. Sometime during your class, pray with the children, thanking God for families and for our special church family. Try a prayer like this:

> Dear God, we thank you for our family that loves us and takes good care of us. We thank you, too, for our church family; we are so happy to be in your church and to be your followers. Help us to be kind and helpful to everyone.

There are several crafts that you could do to reinforce your lesson on the church family:

1. Have a large construction paper leaf for every child with their last names printed on it. Have the children draw the members of their families on the leaves. Make a church family tree mural and have each child put his or her family leaf on the tree. Three-year-olds could use pre-cut pictures from catalogues and glue them on the leaf, as they are not as adept at drawing as the older children.

2. Have the children pick pre-cut pictures (or draw their own) of food that they would give to a hungry family. These could be pasted on a sheet of paper or on a small lunch bag. Explain that feeding a hungry family would be one way of helping someone in our church family.

3. Draw a picture of a priest on a large sheet of paper and have each child draw a picture of himself around the priest. Present the mural to your pastor with the caption, "We are happy to be part of our parish family." (Be sure to label the picture of the priest with your pastor's name so he'll recognize himself!)

This is a very simple lesson on the church family, but you will be surprised to see this small "seed" of church family grow and blossom all year. Your children will develop their own little church family right before your eyes!

Because the family plays such an important role in this lesson, perhaps you would like to send a letter home such as the following:

Dear Parents:
Today we talked about the church family with your child. We told the children that the church family is a group of people who believe in Jesus and try to live the way he did by helping other people and by showing love. Before children can appreciate being members of the church community, they must be aware of what belonging to a family means. This, of course, they have learned from you! We discussed how members of a

family love each other, help each other, speak kindly to each other, etc. Members of a family like to be with each other and do things together. We talked about how the church family is just like our own families and that many families belong to the church. We tried to emphasize that the church is people, not just a building or the priest. We want to make your child feel that he or she is truly a part of our church family.

We also talked about the various "helpers" that are in the church family: priests, sisters, lectors, altar boys, choir and organist, food bank workers, etc. The children need to begin to realize that many people work together in our church family to help get all the jobs done. If the children realize at a young age that many people must work together in the church family, they may be encouraged to help later on.

There are several things that you can do at home to help reinforce this lesson on church family:

1. Make sure that your children know the name of your parish and the names of the priests, sisters and staff members. Encourage them to greet these people when they see them at church.

2. Make some cookies or a dessert to take to the priests or the sisters. Allow your children to help and deliver it together.

3. Always talk positively about the church to your children. All of us have had a bad experience at one time or another, but it is important to encourage a positive attitude about the church to your children at this young age.

4. Encourage your children to act kindly and lovingly toward other people just like Jesus did. Be sure to do this yourself! Remember, example is the best teacher!

BAPTISM

"It was in one Spirit that all of us were baptized into one body. If one member suffers, all members suffer, too; if one member is honored, all members share the joy." 1 Corinthians 12: 13, 26

Baptism, along with confirmation and the eucharist, is a sacrament of initiation. In baptism, we are accepted into the church and become members of the "church family." Before Vatican Council II, the sacrament of baptism was taught as that which removed the "mark" of original sin from the soul. We now realize that original sin is not a "mark," but the inclination toward sin that all humans are born with. Baptism is the sacrament that initiates us into the family that will help us and encourage us to choose the way of Jesus instead of sin, and to truly be children of God by the way we live. As brothers and sisters in the church family, we celebrate with each other, suffer with each other, help and love each other. And with this support, we try to overcome the effects of original sin by living the way humans were intended to live: in the image of God.

By calling baptism our "church birthday," our little ones can more easily understand just what their baptisms were. On our yearly birthdays, we celebrate the fact that we were born into a human family and that we are loved and cared for. On the day of our baptism, we were "reborn" into the church family and accepted into a family where we are also loved and cared for. To impart this understanding to the children, begin your class on baptism with a discussion of birthdays.

A good way to present this theme is to find a story that relates the birth of a new baby and how happy a family is to welcome its new member. Tell the children that their parents were very happy when they were born and each year they remember how happy they still are by celebrating their birthdays. The children could bring pictures of one of their birthdays and these could be shown and discussed. (Be sure to send a note home with the children the week before to ask for the pictures.)

After you talk about birthdays, tell the children that there is a special ceremony that happens to make them members of the church family. Their parents brought them to church when they were just little babies and they were baptized and became members of the church family. You could give the children a short and simple explanation of the ceremony and perhaps use a doll or flannel board figures to demonstrate what happens. Many of the children may be familiar with the ceremony from attending their brother's or sister's baptism. Allow them to tell about it if they are willing. Tell the children that a big candle is lit because this is such a special occasion and that the baby is all dressed in a special white dress or suit. Our baptism is our church birthday because that is the day that we became members of our church family. Have the children bring pictures of their baptisms that everyone may look at and share.

The children are too young to understand the symbolism of the water, the candle, the white garment, the coming of the Spirit, etc. This simple explanation of baptism as joining the church family will lay the foundation for the understanding of these truths at a later date. Remind the children how special it is to be a member of the church family, where people love each other, help each other and live the way God wants them to.

The following songs could be used to reinforce your lesson on baptism.

(Tune: Happy Birthday)
Happy baptism day to you, happy baptism day to you.
You join the church family; what a happy day for you!

(Tune: Frere Jacques)
We are baptized with the water
and candle light, burning bright.
We are very special members of the church.
We are baptized; we love each other.

There are several crafts that you could do to help the children remember their lesson on baptism.

1. If you had the children bring in pictures of their birthdays and their baptisms, you could use the pictures in this way: On half of a sheet of paper, draw the outline of a birthday cake; on the other half, draw the outline of a church. Have the children decorate the cake and color the church in any way they wish. Have them glue or tape their pictures to the appropriate side of the picture. You could also make a class mural using the same idea.

2. Have the children make a birthday cake using "play dough" that you make or purchase. Give them a birthday candle to put on top.

3. The children could decorate a cake-shaped piece of construction paper with tempera paints, crayons, markers, glitter, macaroni, colored cereal, etc. Give them a birthday candle to glue on the cake.

4. Give the children a blown-up balloon and let them draw a face on it. (Permanent markers would work best; wear "paint shirts!") Glue pieces of yarn on it for hair. Use masking tape rolls and tape the faces on a mural or bulletin board labeled, "We are baptized—We are a family!" This project would probably be best accomplished by five-, and possibly, four-year-olds.

5. Make and decorate birthday hats or crowns that the children could wear during the birthday party at snack time.

At snack time you could have a birthday party to celebrate all the children's church birthdays. Ask the parents ahead of time what the date of the child's baptism was and make a little birthday cake shape with the date on it that the child can wear around his neck. Decorate the room as for a birthday party and use special napkins, cups and plates. Any snack that you could put a birthday candle in would be appropriate: cupcakes, brownies, soft cookies, or even fruit would work. Light the candles and sing the song listed above *(Tune: Happy Birthday)*. Be sure to have enough helpers to ensure a safe celebration if you do light the candles. Pray with the children, thanking God for their baptism and their church family. Use a prayer such as the following:

> Dear God, thank you for my baptism and letting me be part of this church family. Thank you for my parents who brought me to church to be baptized and who teach me about you. Help me to be good person in my church family and to be kind and helpful. Thank you for this food we are going to share. Amen.

This lesson presents a wonderful opportunity to educate parents about baptism if they have never attended baptism preparation classes. You could accomplish this by sending home the following letter:

Dear Parents:
Today in class we talked about and celebrated our baptism with the children. We explained to the children that their baptism day is their "church birthday," the day they joined the church family. As they grow older, they will be able to comprehend the significance and symbolism of the water, candles, white clothing, etc. But for now, the above explanation is one they can easily understand.

    Since Vatican Council II, our understanding of baptism and original sin has been clarified. Original sin was once considered a "mark" on the soul that was removed by baptism. We now understand that original sin is not a "mark" but the inclination we have to sin. Baptism makes us members of a church community where we all help each other in this constant struggle against original sin. We encourage and support each other to live the way God intended; in his image. The sacrament initiates us into a community where we work together to attain a fullness of life in Christ. Through the grace of baptism, we share in his death and resurrection and his life is brought out in us through the action of the Holy Spirit. Baptism is a beginning, a commitment to a lifestyle like that of Jesus. And it leads to a full participation in that life through the eucharist.

There are several things you can do at home to reinforce this lesson on baptism.

1. Look at pictures of your child's baptism and talk about the ceremony. Tell them how special it was and how happy everyone was that a new baby had joined the church family.

2. Celebrate your child's "baptism" birthday each year. Set the table with a tablecloth or placemats, flowers, special napkins, and the child's baptism candle. Make a dinner that your child especially likes (even hot dogs or pizza!) and have a small gift for your child. A religious storybook, coloring book, or picture would be appropriate. Show your child pictures of his (her) baptism and the white outfit worn. Celebrate your own baptism birthday too: your child will know that you consider your baptism an important event too!

3. Take your child to church and show him the baptistry. Explain to him (simply) how the ceremony took place and let him look around. This would best be

done when nothing else is scheduled in the church building.

THE MASS

"Where two or three are gathered in my name, there am I in their midst." Matthew 18:20

As young children begin to realize that the church is indeed made up of people, and that they are members of that church, it is important to explain to the children how the church family celebrates together. And, of course, our main family celebration is our weekly participation at Sunday Mass. It is the principal celebration of the church and is a sign of our unity as brothers and sisters in Christ. In addition to being a sign of our unity, going to Mass also promotes and encourages that unity in our weekly gathering of prayer, singing, instruction, and sharing of the eucharist. The Mass, however, is an "adult" service—and even the best children's liturgies do not involve the little ones at a level which they can understand. It is very difficult for preschool and kindergarten age children to understand and assimilate the mysteries and beauty of the liturgy. In our classes, however, we can talk to the children about the Mass as our church family's celebration and our special meal that we eat together each week. The following ideas can be used to present a class session on the Mass to the little ones.

The important concept to always remember in preschool/kindergarten religious education is to build upon what the children have already experienced. In this lesson about the Mass, first talk about how they celebrate family events together. Special meals are one way families come together and share happy events. Talk about how the table is set with a pretty tablecloth, good dishes and silverware, candles and flowers. Remind the children that everyone gets dressed up and a very special meal is cooked for everyone to share. Everyone has a good time; there are stories to share, lots of hugs and kisses, and many things to be happy about. Sometimes families even sing songs together at these special meals. You could use a flannel board and "display" a table with a cloth, dishes, silver, etc. as you discuss these things. You could also actually "set" a table with the children, to be used later in the class for a special snack.

All children have experienced a meal of this sort, at Thanksgiving, Christmas, a birthday, etc. Relate these experiences of celebration to our celebration of the Mass, our church family's special meal. Talk about the altar (table) that is set with good cloths, special dishes (chalice and paten), and candles and flowers. Everyone wears "dressed-up" clothes and special "blessed" food is shared. We have family stories to hear from the Bible and our church family sings together, too. We feel happy to be with our church family and we shake hands and say, "Peace be with you." God knows how much fun it is to celebrate with our church family, too, and that is why we go to Mass. If it is possible, take the children to the church and allow them to look at the areas involved in the celebration of the Mass, i.e., the altar, the lectern, the organ and choir area, etc. Do this when the church is not being used, so that the children are able to talk and are free to look. If this is not possible, use pictures to explain what you are discussing.

There is an excellent book entitled *When Is the Singing Part?* (by Belle Flynn and Peggy O'Connell CSJ, Pflaum Press, 1985), which relates everyday experiences to what the children see and do at Mass. The pictures and text are very well done. You could read this book to the children and talk about it with them. Or you may find a story relating to the theme of family celebrations in the library.

Make music a special part of this class. If your parish has some favorite songs that may be familiar to the children, sing them. The song, "Friends All Gather 'Round" by Carey Landry (from the album *Bloom Where You're Planted*) is an appropriate song to use for this lesson and the children can easily learn the refrain. Or you can use the following song:

(Tune: Twinkle, Twinkle, Little Star)
We go to church to sing and pray
With our church family we will stay
Altar, candles, flowers and song
To our Mass these all belong
A special meal to come and share
To show how much we love and care.

The snack time in this class can be very meaningful. Bring a loaf of bread for the children to share. Buy this from the bakery or bake a loaf of frozen bread dough. The bread should be unsliced. Also, bring a bottle of carbonated or regular grape juice. Have the table set with a cloth, candles, napkins, and flowers. Make the table look special! The children can "process" to the table, carrying the bread and the juice. The song "Friends all Gather 'Round," would be very appropriate here. You could very simply relate the story of the Last Supper to the children. Tell the children that Jesus shared bread and wine at a very special holiday meal with his friends before he went back to heaven. He told them to remember him and do the same thing by having the same kind of meal. That is what we do at Mass. (Be sure the children understand that you are not celebrating Mass in your class!) Tell them that the bread and wine at Mass are specially blessed by the priest. You want them to share this bread and juice together to celebrate the fact that they are all good friends and care about each other. It is not a good idea to tell the children about eating the body and blood of

Jesus; this mystery is well beyond their comprehension and possibly beyond their acceptance. (This reminds me of the time my own preschool-age son was, for once, listening to the words at Mass and specifically to the consecration. After the priest had said, "This is the blood," my son turned to me and said, "Did he say 'blood'? Is he kidding?" It was just a little too much for him.) The children will learn more about the Eucharist during their First Communion preparations later on. At this point, it is best to keep explanations very simple and general.

Pray with the children before your snack, thanking God for their church family and for all the good things that he has provided. Try a prayer such as the following:

Dear God, we thank you for all the people in our church family, and especially for our friends in this class. We thank you for the time we have to celebrate together and for this bread and juice. We share our food together just like Jesus did with his friends. Help us to be kind and helpful like he was. Amen.

Or use the song that appeared earlier in this lesson.

Break the bread in half and show the children the size of the piece to take. Let the children pass the bread and break pieces from the loaf. End your celebration with a prayer, song or with the children shaking hands or giving each other a hug and saying, "I'm glad you are my friend!" or "Thank you for being in my church family!"

There are several craft projects that you could do for this class:

1. Have the children decorate an altar (drawn on paper) with cut-out cloth, candles, flowers, Bible, etc. You could use material scraps or pieces of napkin for the altar cloth, birthday candles, small dried flowers, a square piece of paper with a cross drawn on the front for the book, etc. This

craft would probably work best with the four- and five-year-olds.

2. Young children could select pre-cut mothers, fathers, brothers and sisters (from catalogues) and paste their family around a predrawn altar or onto a picture of the outside of a church. Label the picture, "We Celebrate with Our Church Family."

3. The children could make placemats to be used at their special meal. Use construction paper and allow the children to paste brightly colored shapes on it to make a festive design or decorate any way you please. The children could "fringe" their placemats by snipping the edges.

4. Give each child a piece of paper with a "pew" drawn on it. Let them paste their family into the pew (catalogue pictures). Have the children then paste their family onto a large mural-type picture that has an altar on it. (Perhaps you could decorate it as described in project 1.) Have the children paste their families around the altar and label it, "Our Church Family Celebrates Together!"

This lesson provides a wonderful opportunity to educate parents about the liturgy! There are many people who are not really aware of the liturgy as a celebration and your communication with them could begin to make them realize the importance of their attendance and participation at Mass. Try sending a letter such as the following home after your lesson on the Mass:

Dear Parents:
Today we talked about the Mass with your children. While they are too young to understand the readings, prayers and mysteries of the liturgy, they are able to understand the Mass as a celebration of the church family. We compared the Mass to the special meals that we celebrate with our families at holiday times or on special occasions. We discussed the table that is set

with a beautiful cloth, special dishes, candles and flowers. This was compared to the altar, which is set with a special cloth, candles and flowers and to the special "dishes" we use at Mass (chalice and paten). We talked about all the family stories that are told when families gather and told them that we read stories about our church family from the Bible at Mass. Many families sing songs together at their family celebrations, and our church family sings at their celebrations, too. We always have special food at our meals and we have special food at Mass, too. We give our relatives hugs and kisses at our celebrations and we shake hands at Mass. By comparing the liturgy with events and objects with which the children are familiar, we are better able to help them understand what the Mass is.

It is important that parents have or develop the proper attitude about the liturgy. Do you truly consider it a celebration of your church family, or is it merely an obligation to be fulfilled? The liturgy or celebration of the eucharist is the principal event of our church community. It expresses the unity we have with one another and our active participation also encourages and strengthens that unity. Your attitude regarding the importance of participation at Mass will be passed on and picked up by your little ones much faster by your actions than by what you say. Show your children how important our church family's celebration is to your family, and that attitude will begin to instill a sense of celebration and joy in your children for our beautiful liturgy. Here are some things that you can do to help your child understand the importance of our church family's celebration:

1. Make mealtimes in your family important family gatherings. Do not use meals to reprimand, argue or discipline. Sharing of the days events, talking and

laughing should be the "main fare" at your table during meals.

2. Take your children to church and allow them to look at the altar and the other objects used at Mass. Go during a time when nothing is scheduled at church so that your children may have the freedom to talk and explore.

3. Take your little ones to Mass so that they are familiar with how the church family gathers. While weekly attendance at Mass for your preschool- or kindergarten-age children is a parental decision, they should be taken to Mass occasionally. Holidays are good times to expose your children to the Mass, when the celebrations are especially festive!

THE CHURCH BUILDING

The church building itself is always a fascinating place for the three-, four-, and five-year-old child. The children should understand that the church is the place where the church family comes together to celebrate, to pray, to sing, and to be happy. The explanation that the church is "God's house" or "the place where God lives" is slightly misleading for the little ones. We want the children to know and accept that God is everywhere with them, and by telling them that God lives in the church building, we are implying to them that this is the only place he is. Of course, when they are older, they will understand Jesus' special presence in the eucharist, but for now, a simple explanation of the church being the place where the church family gathers to pray and to be together is best.

The best way to satisfy the children's curiosity and fascination with the church building is to take them on a tour.

This is best accomplished when nothing else is scheduled in the building. A tour done at this time will allow the children freedom of movement and expression without disturbing anyone else. Begin with the outside of the church. In looking at the building, the children can be told that not all churches look alike, just as their house doesn't look just like everyone else's. All Catholic churches have a cross on or by them. The cross is a sign of how much God loves us and that is why it is in front of our church building. Many churches have beautiful stained glass windows that tell us a story or show us a picture about God or his friends, the saints.

Once inside the church, the children will be interested in many things. It is important for them to realize that the church building is a special place, a place where we pray and talk to God, either by ourselves or with other people. They should be encouraged to talk and walk quietly to show how special this place is. Listed below are some of the objects the children will see and how the objects may be explained to them.

1. Holy Water Font When people come into the church, they make the sign of the cross on themsleves with water to remind them of their baptism, the time when they joined the church family. Show the children how to do this and encourage them to try also.

2. Altar and Candles The altar is the church family's table where the special meal is prepared. It is like the table in your house. The candles are lit when the church family is here together because something special is happening, just like a birthday or special dinner.

3. Tabernacle and Sanctuary Light The tabernacle is the place where we keep the special food that we share at Mass. The light is a reminder to us that the church building is a special place where we can talk to God any time.

4. Pulpit This is the place where the priest or lector

stands to read us the stories about God and Jesus from the Bible.

5. Pews These are the seats where all the people sit together to pray, to sing, and to celebrate together.

6. Statues The statues are usually figures of the saints, the special friends of God who are in heaven with him. They are in the church to remind us that God wants us to act just like they did. Point out the statues of Mary and St. Joseph and ask if the children know who they are.

7. Baptistry This is the place where parents bring their babies to be baptized and join the church family. This is where the priest pours the water over the baby's head.

8. Organ and Choir Area This is the organ that the organist plays to help the people sing together. This is where the choir sits and they help all the people in the church to sing their best.

9. Sacristy This is where the priest puts on his special clothes for Mass and where all the things we need in church are kept. If possible, show the children some vestments and vessels used at Mass.

After you have shown the children around the church, allow them to sit in the pews and pray with them. Thank God for their families and for their church family and for the nice building where they can all be together.

CHAPTER 5

Celebrating the Liturgical Year

Celebrating the liturgical year with preschool- and kindergarten-age children is a marvelous way to introduce them to the "life" of the church. For it is in our celebrations, holidays and feasts that we are renewed, refreshed and made joyful in the life we share as Catholic Christians. All life proceeds in a circle, whether we speak of animals, plants, or ourselves; birth to death and new life formed again. And between birth and death, human beings experience many "births" and "deaths" along the way. The baby leaves the womb to begin a new life, suffering and pain lead to a growth of trust in the Lord, death brings new life in eternity. The cycle always prevails.

Our liturgical year carries us through the cycle of living and dying in our spiritual life. At Christmas, our hope is born with the coming of the savior. During Lent, we "die" to those practices or omissions in our lives that keep us from full life in the Lord. Easter brings us the promise of new life forever and the joy of the presence of the risen Lord is with us always. Pentecost fills us with the Spirit and the power to live our Easter lives. Mary and the saints provide us with role models and hope in fulfilling our Christian commitment. And Thanksgiving (while not an "official" part of the church's liturgical year) reminds us to always be thankful and full of praise to the God who has bestowed on us all good gifts. Year after year, we grow and change with the great mysteries of our faith celebrated in the liturgical year.

The little ones will not understand all the religious significance surrounding the holidays and feasts. By celebrating with them on a level they can understand, however, we are introducing them to and involving them in the very life of the community. We are developing attitudes of belonging and also a realization that something important is going on! Children need to realize that the holidays are more than Santa Claus, presents, the Easter bunny, and turkeys. They need to know that God is a very special part of all of our celebrations; and as they grow, they will eventually come to realize that God is the reason for our celebrations!

The following sections will help you celebrate the liturgical year with the three- to five-year-old. The "lessons" have been set up for a classroom situation, but could very easily be revised for use by parents in the home. Each section is set up to include the following:

1. Bible Verse and Introduction This section will provide the catechist or parent with background information about the holiday. It helps the adult focus on the significance of the feast and then provides an adaptation of that focus which will relate to the young child.

2. Suggestions for Class Presentation This section will present ways in which the theme of the lesson may be presented in a manner that the little ones will understand.

Suggestions are made regarding stories and effective methods of storytelling.

3. Songs All of the songs presented in these lessons have been written to be sung to the tunes of childhood songs. This was done to alleviate the need for any musical "expertise." By using these songs, catechists and parents may also be encouraged to write their own!

4. Crafts or Projects Young children learn best by doing. (Actually, we adults seem to do better by "doing" too!) The projects presented are designed to reinforce the lesson while giving the child a feeling of accomplishment, pride and self-worth. A project that requires an inordinate amount of help from an adult will be of little benefit to the child. We are interested in the process and the active involvement of the child in the project—and not how "nice" the project turns out.

5. Parent Letter This letter will help catechists fulfill their purpose of educating the parents as well as the children. Communication with the family is an essential part of the religious education of a young child. The parent letter will list activities that can be done in the home, thus encouraging parents to fulfill their responsibility as the main religious educators of their children.

In using the ideas presented, it is wise to remember that activities may need to be altered to fit the age group and types of children that the catechist or parent is working with. Children are very different from each other; what works in class one year or with one child may "fall flat" when presented to a different group or child. The suggested activities are simply that: suggestions. They are meant to be "springboards," or starting places for your own creativity and imagination.

So, let's begin to celebrate!

CELEBRATING ADVENT

"But you, Bethlehem-Ephrathah, too small to be among the clans of Judah, from you shall come forth for me one who is to be ruler in Israel, whose origin is from of old, from ancient times."
                                                            Micah 5:1

And so the Israelite nation waited for their Messiah. Their Advent was a long, yet hopeful vigil for a king. When Jesus finally did appear, the people did not recognize him and rejected their way to salvation. How fortunate we are! We have been given the gift of faith and understanding and realize that Jesus' kingdom is "not of this world." We who now celebrate Advent contemplate with awe the fact that our God took on a human form, humbled himself beyond imagination and emptied himself to become a creature. He experienced all the human emotions and pain and became one with us in order to redeem us and lead us to his Father. And so each year we wait, wait to celebrate the great feast of his "breaking into" human history and of the Father's greatest gift to us, his Son, Jesus.

Our little ones will certainly not understand the longing of the Jewish people for a Messiah, nor can they comprehend the great significance of the feast of Christmas. However, they can—and do—understand the concept of waiting; and this is the approach we can use to celebrate Advent with the three-, four-, and five-year-old. We can channel their longing and hopefulness for Christmas into a realization that the feast is indeed the birthday of Jesus. And we can try to make them understand that with a little patience, our waiting usually results in good surprises. Following are some ideas that you can use to present a lesson on waiting.

In preparation for this class, wrap small gifts for each child; these should be very simple, such as pieces of candy, small plastic ornaments, packages of gum, etc. At the beginning of class, have each child take a gift and tell them that they must wait until the end of class to open them. Have them put the gifts in a safe place until class is over.

A good type of story to use for this lesson is one that talks about waiting for the birth of a new brother or sister. Your local library, book store, drug store, and hospital are good resources for a story like this. Many of the children will have experienced waiting for a new brother or sister and will be able to share some ways in which their families waited and prepared for the new baby. Be sure to use some pictures, flannel board figures or actual objects (e.g., baby clothes, baby bottles, small silverware, etc.) to enhance your presentation. Also, emphasize how happy everyone is when a new baby is born, even though it is a long time to wait.

Relate this story to the fact that Mary and Joseph had to wait for Jesus to be born too, and they did many of the same things that we do to get ready for their baby. Mary probably made some clothes for Jesus and Joseph probably made a bed for him. Tell the children that Jesus was a very special baby; many people had been waiting a long time for him to be born. They were waiting for a special person to come and teach them all about loving God, and God sent Jesus to them after a long wait. Tell the story of Jesus' birth to the children using pictures or manger figures. Point out how happy Mary and Joseph were when Jesus was born. You may want to give the children the pictures or figures and let them retell the story to you.

Now remind the children that this is the season called Advent, in which we wait for Christmas. This would be a good time to show them an Advent wreath, to explain how it is used and to have a short ceremony. Tell the children that the Advent wreath helps us to wait for Jesus' birthday and to remember how happy we will be when the long wait is over. You can use the following prayers and song during your Advent wreath service:

Week 1 Dear God, Christmas time seems so far away; only one candle to light now! Please help us to be good waiters just like Mary and Joseph were while they waited for Jesus. Help us to do kind things for others while we wait.

Week 2 Dear God, now we can light two candles. Christmas time is getting a little closer. As we decorate our house, help us to remember how Mary and Joseph got things ready for Jesus. Thank you for the fun we are having while we are waiting.

Week 3 Dear God, Jesus' birthday is near; now we can light three candles! There is so much to do to get ready for Jesus' birthday. We want to be good helpers for our moms and dads. Please help us to play nicely and to be good waiters while they are busy getting ready for Christmas.

Week 4 Dear God, our waiting time is almost over; we can light four candles now! Christmas is so close and it's almost time to celebrate. Thank you for sending your best gift to us, your son Jesus, after a long wait. We love you!

Advent time song *(Tune: Twinkle, Twinkle, Little Star):*

See the candles burning bright,
One by one each week we light.
Advent is a time to wait,
Not quite time to celebrate.
When this waiting time is through,
It's Christmas joy for me and you!

Any game in which the children would have to wait their turn would be a good way to "practice" waiting. Bouncing a ball to each child in turn, walking across a balance beam or on a piece of tape on the floor one at a time, etc., would help develop waiting skills. You could also make a snack that you would have to "wait" to eat. Instant pudding or popcorn (wait for it to pop) would be good choices. Or you may cut several apples or bananas to share and the children would have to watch and wait until the pieces were cut and passed out. Be sure to comment on how patiently the children do wait during these activities (if it applies!).

There are several craft projects that the children could do to reinforce this lesson on waiting.

1. Have the children make paper chains out of purple or dark blue paper and instruct them (and their parents) to tear off one link each day until it is Christmas. Have some type of Christmas symbol or picture at the end of the chain such as a star, wreath or nativity scene. (These could be cut from old Christmas cards.)

2. The children could make some type of Advent wreath to take home. Use clay and birthday candles, homemade play dough, styrofoam forms and greens (short pieces cut from an evergreen tree), or construction paper. Send copies of the Advent wreath song and prayers home so that the parents can use them with their children.

3. Construct a manger or a bed for Baby Jesus out of small shoe boxes. Use straw or strips of paper and have the children put a piece of straw in the bed each time they do a kind act for someone. By Christmas, they should have a nice soft bed for Jesus. Instruct the parents to place a small doll or a paper figure of Jesus in the bed on Christmas Eve. (There is a lovely story about this custom, " A Manger Full of Love" in *Waiting for Christmas* by Carol Greene, Augsburg Publishing House, Minneapolis, 1987).

At the end of class, allow the children to open the gifts that you gave them when they came to class. Comment upon how patient they were while waiting and say that now they have a surprise treat!

Be sure to pray with the children, thanking God for the Advent season. Perhaps you could use the following:

Dear God, thank you for helping us to wait and for the good surprises we get when we do wait! We especially thank you for the best surprise of all, your Son, Jesus. Help us to be good waiters until Christmas comes. Amen.

Following is a sample parent letter and Advent calendar that you could send home following your class on Advent. Including an Advent calendar with this letter is a wonderful way to encourage the children and parents to celebrate Advent together in a manner the children can understand.

Dear Parents:
Today we talked about the Advent season in our class. Your child is not able to understand the theological significance of the Advent and Christmas seasons, but he or she certainly understands what waiting is! We talked about waiting for new babies to come into our families and related this to the fact that Mary and Joseph waited and prepared for their baby to come, too. We talked about Advent being the time that we wait for Jesus' birthday and how we can be patient waiters and good helpers.

A good way to help your child wait for Christmas is to do the activities listed on the Advent calendar. Not only will the children enjoy the activities, but they will enjoy even more the time you will spend with them in doing the activities. Your time is something which seems to be in very short supply this time of year, and hopefully, this calendar will provide an impetus to spend a few "fun" minutes each day with your child.

You may be able to begin a family religious tradition by making an Advent wreath and conducting a simple ceremony with your child. There are many books and pamphlets available in religious bookstores to help

SUNDAY	MONDAY	TUESDAY	WEDNESDAY	THURSDAY	FRIDAY	SATURDAY
1. Light the first candle on your Advent wreath.	**2.** Draw the picture of a winter tree.	**3.** Say a prayer for all hungry people in the world.	**4.** Look at some of your baby pictures.	**5.** Look at the stars tonight.	**6.** Learn about Saint Nicholas.	**7.** Talk about Mary, the mother of Jesus.
8. Light the second candle on your Advent wreath.	**9.** Start making a Christmas gift for someone special.	**10.** Make some paper snowflakes for decorations.	**11.** Play a game with your family.	**12.** Look at pictures of your last birthday party.	**13.** Have some hot chocolate and popcorn with your family.	**14.** Take a winter walk with your family.
15. Light three candles (include pink) on your Advent wreath.	**16.** Say a prayer for all sick people.	**17.** Help make Christmas cookies.	**18.** Take some Christmas cookies to an elderly friend.	**19.** Make a Christmas card for a special person.	**20.** Sing your favorite Christmas carol. NOEL	**21.** Read the story of Jesus' birthday.
22. Light four candles on your Advent wreath.	**23.** Make a birthday card for Jesus.	**24.** Make a birthday cake for Jesus.	**25.** Merry Christmas! Sing "Happy Birthday" to Jesus.	RELIGION TEACHER'S JOURNAL NOV./DEC. 1985		

ADVENT CALENDAR

you do this. Even if your child does not fully understand the significance of the Advent wreath ceremony, he (she) will understand that something important is going on; and all children love candles and singing!

It is also a good idea to have a story book about the nativity that you and your child can read together. Having plastic or paper manger scene figures of their own will encourage the children to remember this special story through play.

I know that you are all very busy at this time of year, but don't forget to prepare yourself and your family to celebrate the true "reason for the season." Blessings on you and your families!

CELEBRATING CHRISTMAS

"The people who walked in darkness have seen a great light; upon those who dwelt in the land of gloom a light has shone. You have brought them abundant joy and great rejoicing. For a child is born to us, a son is given us; upon his shoulder dominion rests. They name him Wonder-Counselor, God-Hero, Father-Forever, Prince of Peace." Isaiah 9:1-2, 5

Such grand titles for a little one! Yet the feast of Christmas is a celebration of the birthday of a child, a child destined to do great things. The fact that our God entered the human race as a helpless child and chose to grow and mature as we all do, in order to identify with our joy, pain, and suffering is an awesome thought that deserves much meditation. For by coming as a child, Jesus allows us to identify with him and truly follow him in his way to the Father. He shows us that membership in his kingdom and salvation are "humanly" possible and gives us great hope and strength on our journey to his Father and eternal life.

Our three-, four-, and five-year-olds are not able to understand the entire significance of Christmas, but they do understand the celebration of birthdays and the importance of the one who is celebrating the special day. All the children know what a birthday party is! We can use their experience of birthdays to explain and relate the importance of Christmas as the celebration of Jesus' birthday. In this way we can also channel their excitement about Christmas toward a Christian attitude of a celebration of Jesus and away from the materialism and commercialism that is rampant at this time of year. So, plan to have a birthday party for Jesus for your presentation of a Christmas lesson.

The atmosphere of your class area plays an important role in setting the mood for this lesson. Decorate the room as you would for a birthday party, using balloons and crepe paper streamers. The children could decorate party hats or crowns as they arrive or you could have them ready for the children to wear. ("Crowns" can be very simply made of construction paper and gummed stars or stickers.) Have Christmas music playing as the children arrive.

Begin class by asking the children why they think that the room is decorated as it is. Lead them into a discussion about birthdays, beginning with how happy their parents and relatives were when they were born. People came to see them and brought presents for them. (If you have children of your own, relate your own experience of how happy you were when your children were born.) Explain how special it is for their family and friends to celebrate their birthdays; it's their way of saying how glad they are that you were born! Ask the children how they celebrate birthdays at home, i.e., special food, cake, candles, balloons, decorations, etc. Use pictures if possible during this discussion, either from magazines, children's books or your own family picture album. (With a little advance planning, you could ask all of the children to bring in pictures of themselves at one of their birthday parties and use these in your discussion.)

Following this discussion, ask the children if they know whose birthday we celebrate on Christmas Day. Tell the children the story of the nativity, using large colorful pictures, flannel board figures or puppets. (Puppets can be made by using coloring book figures. Color the figures, mount them on heavy paper and attach them to paint stirrers.) It is good to have actual Nativity figures that the children can handle (plastic or paper). Give the pieces to the children and let them "place" them in the stable or scene as you tell the story. They can also retell the story using the same figures.

Tell the children that Mary and Joseph were so happy when Jesus was born, just as their parents were when they were born. The shepherds and wise men came to visit and brought presents to Jesus just like their friends and relatives did when they were born. Try to make the children understand that Christmas is a special birthday because all of us get to celebrate: we receive gifts, we visit our friends, we have special foods and beautiful decorations. How wonderful that God sent the son to live with us and now everyone can celebrate his birthday! Be sure to tell the children that Jesus did not stay a baby, just as they are not babies anymore. He grew up to be a great teacher and leader and showed all of us how to love God and each other better. We remember his birthday because of the great things he did when he grew up to be a man. He showed us how to love people, how to be kind to everyone and how to help people. You can end the discussion by asking the children to join you in thanking God for Jesus and for being able to share in the celebration of Jesus' birthday.

Make up your own prayer or you can use the following songs:

(Tune: Twinkle, Twinkle, Little Star)
At Christmas time we celebrate
Jesus' birthday, he is great!
Showed us how to love and care,
Taught us that we all should share.
Thank you, God, for your own Son,
And for all his birthday fun!

(Tune: Twinkle, Twinkle, Little Star)
Jesus' birthday time is here
Time for love and time for cheer.
Christmas means to celebrate
After such a long, long wait.
Share God's love with all you know
Let your Christmas spirit show!

(Tune: Mary Had a Little Lamb)
Jesus was born on Christmas day,
  Christmas day, Christmas day,
Jesus was born on Christmas day,
  God's gift of love to us.

There are many, many crafts that you could do with the children for this lesson. Some are listed here but use your imagination (or craft books from the library!)

1. Have a pre-drawn birthday cake and let the children decorate it with macaroni, glitter, popped popcorn, colored cereal, tinsel, stickers, stars, etc. You may wish to give each child a small birthday candle to glue on the cake. Print "Happy Birthday, Jesus!" on the cake or at the top of the paper.

2. Have the children decorate Christmas trees or ornaments in the same manner as in 1.

3. The children could glue pre-cut nativity figures onto a nativity scene and color them. You could also use a picture of Jesus in the manger which the children could color and then glue straw into the manger, using real or "paper" straw.

4. Cut drinking straws into various lengths and have the children use them to glue "branches" on each side of a pre-drawn trunk to make a Christmas tree. The trees could be decorated if desired using glitter, small pieces of tinsel, red cinnamon candies, gummed stars, etc.

5. Cut Christmas shapes out of potato halves and allow children to make their own wrapping paper by making prints on tissue paper or newsprint using tempera paints. (Put sponges or folded paper towels in styrofoam trays and pour on small amounts of paint.) The children could also decorate a square box-shaped piece of construction paper and put a construction paper or real bow on it.

6. If you have had the children bring in a picture of

themselves at one of their birthday parties, you could make a class collage or poster. In the middle of the paper, glue a picture of the nativity scene (from an old Christmas card or coloring book) and put the children's pictures all around it. Label the poster, "We Celebrate Birthdays!" or "Thank You, God, for Birthdays!"

Celebrate Jesus' birthday in your class with a special cake and candles, ice cream (if possible) and milk or juice. Use festive birthday napkins, plates, cups, and a tablecloth. (Parents would probably be glad to donate these.) Be sure to sing "Happy Birthday" to Jesus and thank God for the snack you will share. Play Christmas music while the children are eating. If you can manage it, you could have the snack at the end of class and invite the parents to share in Jesus' birthday party. We can all use a reminder what Christmas is really about and this is a nice way to involve parents in your lesson; they'll reinforce the message at home!

To enable your parents to carry the message home, the following parent letter could be used:

Dear Parents:

Today in class we celebrated Jesus' birthday with a party, complete with cake, ice cream, and decorations! We are hoping to remind the children—and you!—that the reason for celebration at Christmas time is the realization that our God came to live with us. Think of it! Our mighty God came to stay with us, came to share our joys, our emotions, our sufferings, our pain so that he could show us that it is humanly possible to attain eternal life with him and his Father. Your little ones will not quite understand all the theological reasons why we celebrate Christmas, but they should be aware that it is a religious feast and not just a time to get many, many presents. As parents, you are the ones who will set the tone for the holiday, who will teach your children just what Christmas is all about. It is very difficult not to get caught up in the materialism and commercialism of the holiday but as Christian parents we need to teach our children that Christmas is a time of thanksgiving, of sharing, of giving, and finally, of receiving.

Following is a list of things that you could do at home to help celebrate Christmas with your little ones:

1. Together with your children, look at pictures that you took when they were born. Tell them the story of their birthdays; what the weather was like, what time of the day it was, who took you to the hospital, how happy you were when they were born, who came to see you in the hospital, etc. Relate this to the nativity story of Jesus' birthday.

2. Be sure to make a birthday cake for Jesus and sing "Happy Birthday" on Christmas Day. Don't forget to let your children blow out the candles!

3. Decide on some way to share what you have with those less fortunate. Take your little ones shopping and let them help you choose some canned goods for a food pantry, a small toy, gloves, hat, slippers, or scarf for a disadvantaged child, etc. You could also make some cookies and take them to an elderly or housebound neighbor, make a picture or card and take it to a nursing home, etc. When you do any of these things, be sure to tell your children that Jesus taught us to be kind to others and to share what we have with poor people.

4. Try to monitor the amount and type of television programming that your children are watching. So much of the "I want" comes from what children see on television. Turn the set off and spend some time with your children reading, doing puzzles, walking, baking,

etc. The best present you can give your children for Christmas is *you* — your time, your undivided attention, your love.

A joyful and blessed holiday to you and your families!

CELEBRATING VALENTINE'S DAY

"This is how all will know you as my disciples: by your love for one another." John 13:35

Although Valentine's Day is not a "religious" holiday, it is the day that celebrates the quality that distinguishes us as followers of Jesus: love. As Catholic Christians, we have many distinguishing traditions and practices, but it is our ability and willingness to love God and others in a concrete, active way that is the true mark of our belief. This is the characteristic, the "practice," that is of the upmost importantance to be passed to our children. In our classes celebrating this holiday then, we want the children to realize that the love they feel and share with their families and friends is a wonderful gift of God and that it is our "job" to share that love with everyone.

Love—this simple word means so much to all of us, yet is almost impossible to define. Our young children will not readily understand definitions anyway, but we can describe love for them by naming experiences in which they have received love. In our classes, we also strive to create communities where the children have the opportunity to feel and to share love. These experiences of being loved and showing love for others are necessary to understanding and believing that God loves us, because God's love for us is given and received through other people. Jesus came and lived with us to show us what God's love is like. What a wonderful gift to celebrate with the children! And a class for Valentine's Day should be just that, a celebration!

If possible, decorate your class area in red and white, using construction paper hearts, balloons, crepe paper, flowers, etc. The children will know it's a special day (and a special lesson!) by the festive appearance of the room. You may want to display pictures of love "happening:" mothers/fathers with babies, families playing or working together, friends sharing, grandparents, parish or church scenes, Jesus and the children, etc. These pictures could also be used in a presentation to describe love for the children and help them to realize that they are loved.

There are many stories that you could tell the children to illustrate this theme; the library would be a good source for these stories. Any story relating love between family members, friends, animal friends, community helpers, etc. would be appropriate. Explain to the children that this special feeling called love is a gift from God, who wants us to share it with everyone. Talk about some ways that the children can show love, i.e., hugs, kisses, sharing, listening, and waiting patiently.

You may want to tell the children the story of the Good Samaritan. Because our little ones do not understand what a Samaritan or a Levite is, it would be a good idea to paraphrase the story to relate to the experiences of the children. Remember, keep it simple! Try a story like this:

> You all remember who Jesus is, right? He is God's Son and was born on Christmas. When Jesus grew up to be a man like your dad, he told stories to the people to teach them how to be kind and to love everyone. One of the stories he told went something like this.
>
> "One day, Jimmy, who was just about your age, was

riding his bike. A group of big kids came by and started teasing Jimmy. One of the big kids knocked him off of his bike and then they all ran away. Jimmy's leg was cut and his foot was stuck in the bike and he couldn't go home. He started to cry. An important man in a suit carrying a briefcase came by and saw Jimmy crying. But he was very busy and had to hurry to get to work so he rushed right by. And then a lady walked by with a bag of groceries, but she was in a hurry to get home and put her groceries away, so she rushed by and didn't stop to help.

"Then Paulie came by. Jimmy didn't like Paulie very much because he was from a faraway country and looked different; and Jimmy thought Paulie talked funny, too. Jimmy had never been very nice to Paulie and usually went into the house when he saw him coming down the street so he wouldn't have to play with him. Jimmy never thought Paulie would help him. But as soon as Paulie saw Jimmy lying on the ground, he came over to help. Then Paulie ran up the street to get Jimmy's mother, who came right away and carried Jimmy home. Paulie helped bring Jimmy's bike home."

Which one of the people who came by showed Jimmy the most love? Do you think that Paulie should have helped Jimmy, since Jimmy had never been very nice to him?" Tell the children that Jesus wants us to be just like Paulie in the story. Jesus always treated people kindly and he showed love to everyone, even if they weren't very nice to him. God wants us to follow Jesus and act the same way. You can, of course, use pictures, puppets, or flannel board figures to enhance your presentation of the Good Samaritan story.

As a sign of love for each other, ask the children to hold hands. Have them close their eyes and pray with them, using a prayer like the following:

Dear God, please help us to love each other just like Paulie in the story. Help us to be kind to everyone, even when they are not so kind to us. Thank you for sending Jesus to teach us the way to love everyone. And thank you for Valentine's Day, the holiday when we celebrate your gift of love. Amen.

You could also use the following song for your prayer to reinforce the theme of your Valentine's lesson.

(Tune: Jesus Loves Me)
Jesus loves me, this I know
and he came to earth to show
how we should be kind and care
and love all people everywhere.
Yes, Jesus loves me, yes, Jesus loves me
Yes, Jesus loves me,
and I will share his love.

Following are some ideas that you could use for craft projects for your Valentine's class. (Make sure the children know that the heart is a sign of love.)

1. Show the children how to cut hearts from a folded sheet of construction paper. Have them cut two red hearts and glue them to a piece of pink or white construction paper, point to point so that they resemble a butterfly. The children could cut smaller pink or white hearts to decorate the wings (or you could have them pre-cut for the younger children). Have the children add antennae using pipe cleaners or strips of construction paper and eyes using crayons.

2. Have the children make placemats for your party or to use at home. Let them decorate a white, red, or pink placemat with contrasting color hearts. You can use construction paper if you don't have placemats and let the children "fringe" the ends by making small cuts with their scissors.

3. Let the children make a Valentine card for their parents or grandparents. Draw a heart on a folded sheet of construction paper and let the children use colored cereal to make "lace" around the heart. A duplicated verse and a picture of the child could be put inside.

4. Let the children make a heart collage by using heart-shaped pieces of sponge and tempera paint. Have them dip the sponges into paint-soaked paper towels or a sponge (on a plastic meat tray). Use red paint and pink or white construction paper.

5. Make a heart wreath. Cut the center out of a small paper plate and let the children glue pink and red hearts around the rim. Help the children hang a small heart in the middle saying "God helps me show love" and attach a yarn loop or some type of hanger at the top. Tell the children that they can hang their wreath somewhere at home to remind themselves and their families to show love to each other.

Of course, the topic of love is not something we reserve for Valentine's Day. Jesus did not simply tell stories about loving; he showed us how to love, to the point of giving his life for us. The children in your class will learn the most about love by your example and by the way you treat them, talk to them, and love them. You will be "teaching" about love every time your class meets. The concept that parents are "teaching" their children about love every day by the way they treat their children and everyone around them is so important for parents to understand. The letter below could be sent home to parents following your class for Valentine's Day. (If you used the story of Paulie, the "Good Samaritan," you may want to send a copy of that home so that the parents will know what the children heard.)

Dear Parents:
Today we celebrated Valentine's Day with your children. The emphasis in our class was on love as being a

wonderful gift that God gave us. The children heard a paraphrased version of the Good Samaritan story (attached) and we talked about how Jesus told stories and showed us how to be kind and to love everyone, even if they are not always kind to us.

It is so important to realize that you are "teaching" your children about love every day, by the way that you love them. Do you speak kindly to them, hug them, hold them, look at them when you are talking to them, read to them, spend time with them, lovingly discipline them? Do you show love to those around you also, even if you do not feel that you have always been treated kindly or fairly? Remember that your children will learn about love by what you do and not just by what you say. You must be a loving person, following Jesus' example, if you want your child to become a loving and caring follower of Jesus. This is a "tall order" sometimes, but one that we are called to, as Jesus instructed: "Love one another as I have loved you." Below are some activities that you can do at home to continue this lesson on love:

1. Determine to spend time with your children, time that they have your undivided attention. Read a story, take a walk, play a game, or even watch Sesame Street together!

2. Bake and decorate some heart-shaped cookies with your child. Take them to a grandparent, elderly friend or shut-in.

3. Take a few minutes of quiet time each day and reflect on your attitude toward others and how you can truly be a more loving person. Read the gospels to discover how Jesus treated those around him and "do likewise!"

CELEBRATING LENT

"Reform your lives! The reign of God is at hand." Matthew 3:2
"I am the way, the truth and the life; no one comes to the Father but through me." John 14:6

For adults, the season of Lent encourages us to spend some time re-evaluating our lives in terms of how well we are living the gospel message. Are we true disciples, living and loving as Jesus did and charged us to do? Lent is a wonderful opportunity for us to continue our conversion and our journey to the Father by trying to live our lives more fully in the manner Jesus taught us. Through this re-evaluation and introspection we discover "problem" areas in our lives, situations in which we have sinned through action or omission. In the sacrament of reconciliation, we indeed reconcile ourselves with God and our community and resolve to live more fully in accord with Jesus' teachings.

Our little ones cannot appreciate or take part in this re-evaluation and reconciliation. In fact, they are not really aware of the morally right and wrong ways to do things. For them, the "right" way to act is that which will satisfy their own wishes. Things are "wrong" if they are corrected or caught. They will advance to more mature systems of morality as they grow, but how do we make Lent meaningful to preschool and kindergarten children? Lent as the season of discipleship can be presented in a manner that the children will understand. If we think of discipleship as being "friends with Jesus," we can begin to build this relationship between the children and Jesus. This is also a very positive way to dwell on the meaning of Lent. Instead of concentrating on the "bad" things that we shouldn't do, we emphasize the good and proper ways in which followers of Jesus act.

Before we can begin to talk about being friends with Jesus, we must be sure that our little ones have a basic idea of what a friend is. This is important because they must have and be friends with people they can see before they are able to think about being friends with someone they can't see. And their ideas of friendship will differ, even among the three-, four-, and five-year-olds. Three-year-olds are just beginning to realize that other people exist besides themselves; they are still quite self-centered. Four-year-olds are are a little more advanced in socialization skills and are more aware of other people. Five-year-olds, especially those in kindergarten, are much more aware of people and friends because of their school experiences. So don't be discouraged if the children aren't fully aware of all that friendship entails. Remember, we are "foundation builders" and are presenting concepts that will be re-presented and re-taught each year. But we want the children to begin to know Jesus as their loving friend and not some far-away person that merely watches everything that they do.

You may want to present a lesson on friends before you talk about being a friend of Jesus. Ideas for a lesson on friends were presented in the "Lessons for Little People" column in the October 1986 issue of *Religion Teacher's Journal* (Twenty-Third Publications) and many of the preschool and kindergarten textbooks include such a lesson. In talking to the children about their friends, be sure to discuss how much they like to do the same things their friends do; act the same way, play the same games, eat the same snacks, etc. They feel happy with their friends and help each other if they are in trouble.

To begin your lesson on "discipleship" (being friends with Jesus) and Lent, first explain to the children that each year we spend forty days just before Easter thinking about how God wants us to love each other. At Easter time we celebrate "new life," so to get ready for Easter, we try to think of new ways that we can do what God wants us to do. How do we know what we should do or how we should act? God sent Jesus to live on earth to show us how he wants us to treat other people and show God's love to them. Remind the children that the baby Jesus whose birthday we celebrated at Christmas time grew up to be a man just like their fathers. He spent his life showing people how to be good friends to each other and how to treat everyone kindly. Many people loved Jesus and wanted to be like him because he made people happy and was such a good friend to everyone. He especially loved children. You may want to tell the story of Jesus and the children; perhaps you could relate it in this way:

> Jesus was resting under a big tree where it was shady and cool. He was very tired because he had been talking to lots of people all day about God and helping them if they were sick. Some children came to see Jesus; they knew he was very kind and they wanted to sit on his lap and talk to him. Jesus' helpers said to the children: "Go away now and let Jesus rest. He is very tired and doesn't have time for you now." But Jesus heard his helpers and said, "Don't send the children away. I love to hold them and talk to them. And I always have time for children." And he held out his arms to them. The children laughed and ran over to Jesus. They sat on his lap and hugged him and talked to him. I'll bet they even sang some songs together! Jesus told his helpers, "If you want to be my friends and follow me, then you will have to be happy and love me like the children do." Then the children said goodbye to Jesus and went home with their moms so that Jesus could rest.

Tell the children that they will want to act like Jesus and do the things he did, just as they want to do the things that their other friends do. He told the people to "come and be my friends and make people happy the way I do." You may also tell the children that the Bible has many stories in it that tell us about Jesus and the way he treated other people. Jesus wants us to act just like he did. Perhaps you can use the following parable to show the children how Jesus acted.

> One day, a large crowd of people came to hear Jesus tell stories and talk about how much God loved them. He was such a good storyteller that they listened to him for a long time, and then it was getting close to supper time. There were no stores close by and no such thing as McDonalds where they could buy supper. Many of the people were hungry and had no food. Jesus had some food that a boy had given him—how nice of that little boy to share his food with Jesus! Before Jesus ate the food, he said a prayer to his Father in heaven (just as we pray before we eat our meals to thank God for the food) and then he started to share his food with the other people around him.
>
> Some of the people in the crowd had brought food with them, and when they saw Jesus sharing his food they decided to share their food, too. How happy everyone was! It was like a big picnic! There was plenty to eat for all the people and there were twelve baskets of food left over! Jesus made the people happy by being a good friend and sharing his food. And the people wanted to be like Jesus, so they made other people happy by sharing their food, too.

In using either the story of Jesus and the children or the story of loaves and fishes, it would be a good idea to use some type of visual aids with the presentation. Pictures, flannel board figures or puppets would help the children better remember the stories. There is an excellent filmstrip called "Jesus Lives" (Benziger Publishing Company) in their teacher's resource kit for the *Come, Children, Hear Me* kindergarten program. This would be an excellent resource for this lesson.

Tell the children that we are Jesus' friends, too. We want to be just like he was and to make people happy by sharing and doing nice things for others. You can discuss some simple ways that they can do this, such as sharing toys, talking nicely to each other, helping at home, etc. We also need to make the children realize that they will feel good and be happy by helping others and by acting the way Jesus wants us to. Jesus told us that if we help others, we will be a hundred times happier ourselves. You may want to show some pictures of smiling children and tell the little ones that they will look and feel this way if they are like Jesus.

Be sure to pray with the children, using a prayer such as the following:

Thank you, God, for your Son, Jesus, who showed us how to be such good friends and who is our friend, too. Please help us to be just like he was, kind to everyone we meet and good helpers, too. Amen.

You could also use the following songs with the children:

(Tune for both: Frere Jacques)
1. I love Jesus, yes I do,
   He's my friend, he's my friend
   And I'll try to do things just the way that he did
   show my love, do kind things.

2. Treat friends kindly, treat friends kindly
   Show God's love, show God's love
   The Bible tells us always to do kind things for others
   Show God's love, show God's love.

The following are some craft ideas that you can use with this lesson on Lent and discipleship:

1. Have the children make a lenten chain using strips of purple construction paper. Tell the children, "Each day when you tear off a link, you should do one nice thing for someone and act like Jesus did. When you are done, you will have done 40 new things to get ready for Easter!" Put a butterfly at the end of the chain. (The butterfly is a symbol of the resurrection and new life. See Easter lesson.) You will need to inform the parents how to use the chain.

2. You can make "happy" faces, showing how the children will make others look by being like Jesus and how they will look, too! On construction paper or paper plates, use dried beans or peas, macaroni, popped popcorn, miniature marshmallows, colored cereal, etc., and yarn pieces (for hair) to construct happy faces. (For three- and four-year-olds, you may want to indicate by small x's or dots the outline of the eyes, nose, and smiling mouth.) The children could also spread peanut butter on a slice of bread and use raisins to make a happy face; this would be a great snack!

3. Give the children a piece of drawing paper that has a picture of Jesus on one half (from a coloring book or card) and blank on the other side. Have three- and four-year-old children paste pre-cut pictures of their choice showing kindness and love (ways Jesus acted) on the blank side. Kindergarten children could draw a way they could be a friend to someone. Label the picture, "We Show Love as Jesus Did."

4. In preparation for this project, trace one of each of the children's hands on sheets of paper and cut out the drawings. Staple a paper towel on the hand. Have the childen cut out large circles to represent dinner plates and glue to a piece of construction paper. Give each child their hand with the towel and let them glue the hand to the construction paper plate to represent helping by drying the dishes. You could label this picture, "We Are Helpers Like Jesus."

5. Make some type of card or favor and send it to a nursing home or children's floor at the hospital. Remind the children how happy the people will be who receive their gift.

In this lesson, we are trying to instill the attitudes of loving and caring that Jesus expects of his disciples. This concept can be positively reinforced all year, reminding children how "friends of Jesus act and treat each other." Remember, your example is the best lesson you can teach. If you act the way Jesus did and you are a friend of Jesus, the children will imitate you. It is necessary that the parents realize how important their example in the home is, too. Here is a letter you could use to encourage parents to participate in this lenten season of discipleship:

Dear Parents:

Today in class we talked with the children about the season of Lent. We explained to the children that during the forty days before Easter we look for new ways to act like Jesus and try to be more loving and better helpers. We told the children that they are special friends of Jesus and that they should act just as he did in showing love to other people. This will make the people they love and help happy, and the children will be happier, too!

This discussion is based upon the period of reflection and introspection in which the church engages each lenten season. As adults, we are encourged to look upon our own lives to discover how well we are fulfilling our mission as disciples of Jesus. How closely are we living according to the values he set forth in his teachings in the gospels? We look to the "problem areas" in our lives and discover sins we may have committed through action or omission. Through the sacrament of reconciliation, we re-establish our friendship with Jesus and our community and resolve to live more fully as followers of Jesus' way. The little ones do not understand the moral implications of sin or the process of reconciliation, so we concentrate on ways that they can be followers of Jesus in a manner they can understand.

As parents, the most important "job" we have to do is to live an exemplary Catholic Christian life; and that is not the easiest task sometimes! But it is only through observation of your way of living that your children will "catch" the faith and lifestyle of a follower of Jesus. You can lecture and say all you wish, but if you do not "practice what you preach," your words will go unheeded. So this Lent, resolve to become better examples for your children. But not just for your children; re-establishing and strengthening your friendship with Jesus is the best thing you can do for yourself!

Try some of these activities at home to encourage your family's participation in this lenten season:

1. As a family, discuss ways that each person could be a better follower of Jesus. Have each person decide on one way that they are going to try to do this for the forty days of Lent. Perhaps you could make a chart using stickers or stars and have family members "reward" themselves daily as they accomplish what they promised to try.

2. As a family, collect canned goods for a food pantry. Instead of eating dinner in a restaurant, use the money as a donation to a food bank, soup kitchen or food pantry.

3. (Insert directions for use of your lenten chain if you decided to use it as a craft project.)

4. Talk to your child about what it means to be friends with other people and with Jesus. If your child does not have a picture of Jesus, perhaps you could go

together to a religious store and pick one out. (Choose a picture that will appeal to your child. Some lovely Frances Hook pictures have been produced on plaques at a reasonable price.)

CELEBRATING EASTER

"I am the resurrection and the life: whoever believes in me, though he should die, will come to life." John 11:25-26

New life—Jesus always promised everlasting life to those who believed in him and lived according to his words. Easter is the greatest feast of the church in which we celebrate the completion of the redemptive act and the hope of eternal life at the end of our earthly lives. The resurrection is central to our faith and belief. Yet, the depth of understanding needed to comprehend the spiritual mysteries of Easter is far beyond the capabilities of three-, four,- and five-year-olds. How, then, do we celebrate this great feast with our little ones?

One very good approach to Easter for young children is to emphasize and celebrate the "new life" that they see, hear and smell all around them at Easter time. We spend the weeks before Easter presenting classes with themes such as light, water, soil, seeds and planting, and growing. We can explain to the children that these are all the "materials" God uses to give us new life. We can talk about eggs and the baby chicks that hatch from them. Baby bunnies and lambs are born in the springtime. The birds begin to sing again and the grass smells so good! This presentation is another example of why our preschool and kindergarten religious education programs are called "religion readiness" programs. We take the everyday experiences of the child and their concrete way of looking at things and make the child aware of the good gifts that God has given us. Later in their development, they will understand the theological significance of the feast.

Many books and stories, available at the library and even at drug and grocery stores at this time of year, present this theme of new life. Stories about spring, hatching baby chicks and birds, bunnies, seeds and growing plants, etc., are appropriate. Be sure to be enthusiastic and joyful when you present these lessons on new life. (For those of us who live in the snow belt, this will not be difficult to do!) Your enthusiasm will be caught by the children.

There is one new life theme which every young child should be taught and that is the story of the butterfly. There is no more appropriate way to present the new life of Easter than through the explanation of the marvelous and mysterious process that transforms a homely caterpillar into a beautiful butterfly. The caterpillar buries himself in his cocoon and appears to die; yet later appears as a beautiful butterfly. It is the same life, but a different form. Not only does it take on new life, but it pollinates flowers and shares its beauty as it flies from flower to flower in its new form. There are many stories and books available to present the butterfly story. *The Very Hungry Caterpillar* by Eric Carle is a delightful story that presents the butterfly saga in an appealing way for young children. This story also lends itself to dramatization, especially if you have some older students or parents that might be interested in helping present the lesson.

The crucifixion and death of Jesus are vital and important parts of the Easter story. However, we do not usually present these events to young children as the story may frighten them; also, they cannot understand the significance of Jesus' suffering and death. If you have been speaking of Jesus' goodness and kindness in your classes, the little ones may wonder why anyone would want to hurt him. They are simply not able to understand the political and social situation of Jesus' time. Children do experience death, however, either of loved ones or pets, and the story of the butterfly can be used to help explain this event to them.

I had the occasion to do this when my grandfather died. Naturally, I was concerned about what my four- and six-year-old would think when they went to the funeral home. I knew they were familiar with the story of the butterfly so this is what I told them. I said that the body that they would see was like the cocoon that the butterfly left behind. "Papa" had gone off to his new life with God just like the butterfly flies off to his new life. We are sad because Papa is not living with us any more, but we are happy, too—because he is living his new life with God. He would never be sick or hurt again in his new life with God. The boys accepted this readily and had an easier time dealing with the reality of their great-grandfather's death. The butterfly story is a nonthreatening and simple explanation of death that the little ones can relate to and understand in their own way. "Grandpa, Jimmy and the Dragonfly" is a good filmstrip to use to teach little children about death (available from Twenty-Third Publications).

Death as a theme for a class of three-, four-, or five-year-olds is not recommended. In presenting this theme to a class, there may be a family situation that you are not aware of and your discussion may elicit a reaction that you are not prepared to handle. It would be better to send some information home to the parents (such as the butterfly story and its application to death) and let the parents handle the subject in their own way.

As adults, we understand the beautiful analogy of the butterfly, resurrection and new life of Jesus Christ. And we can also understand the comparison of this event to the fact that a seed must "die" before new growth will appear.

These comparisons will be "lost" on the little ones because they cannot deal with abstraction. However, by emphasizing their "real life" experiences with these topics in their early years, the children will eventually understand them in a much deeper sense. So just enjoy celebrating "new life" with your little ones, knowing that you are "planting seeds" for future understanding.

Pray with the children, thanking God for new life in spring. You may want to use a litany-type prayer with them, such as the following. Their reponse could be, "Thank you, God," or "We love you, God."

> Dear God, we thank you for all the wonderful gifts you have given us in spring. There is new life all around us!
> For baby bunnies and lambs, we say, R. Thank you, God.
> For new green plants and leaves, we say, R.
> For the birds that are singing again, we say, R.
> For the grass that smells so good, we say, R.
> For the caterpillars and the beautiful butterflies, we say, R.
> For the pretty spring flowers, like the crocus and daffodil, we say, R. Etc.

You may want to sing one of the following songs with your children to celebrate the new life of Easter:

(Tune: Frere Jacques)
Spring is new life, spring is new life
Winter's gone, winter's gone.
Baby chicks are peeping, caterpillars creeping
Spring is here, thank you, God!

(Tune: Mulberry Bush—use appropriate actions)
This is the way we rake the ground, rake the ground,

rake the ground
This is the way we rake the ground, so early in the springtime.
This is the way we plant the seed, etc.
This is the way the sun shines down, etc. *(put arms over head in a circle)*
This is the way the rain comes down, etc. *(wiggle fingers)*
This is the way the plant pops up, etc.

(Tune: Ten Little Indians)
Alleluia, spring is here.
Alleluia, spring is here.
No more cold and no more winter!
Thank you, God, for spring!

You could also have the children pretend that they are seeds that have been planted in the ground. Have them roll up in little balls and gradually stand up and "grow." Be sure to have the rain come down and the sun shine on them! They could also pretend to be "very hungry caterpillars," as in the book mentioned above, and go through all the actions to become beautiful butterflies. There is a very simple action that the children can do which will explain the cross to them. Have them stand with their arms extended at their sides at shoulder height. Their bodies will form a cross. Show them the cross shape. Tell the childen that "God loves you this much," and show them with your arms. Tell the children that whenever they see a cross shape, it reminds them of how much God loves them.

You can use one of the following crafts to help the children remember their lesson on new life:

1. Make egg carton caterpillars. Cut the egg carton sections in half (six each) and give each child one section. Have the children paint the cartons with glue and attach cotton balls or short pieces of yarn so that their caterpillars look

fuzzy. Use black pipe cleaners for antennae and small yellow circles for eyes.

2. Make clothespin butterflies, using a 12-inch square of multi-colored tissue paper or a colored napkin, a wooden non-clip clothespin, and a black pipe cleaner. Insert the paper into the wooden clothespin and gather firmly to form the wings. Wrap the pipe cleaner around the head of the clothespin to form the antennae.

3. The children can make pussy willow stems by gluing puffed wheat, cotton balls, or miniature marshmallows to drawn stems. Using light blue construction paper for a background makes a pretty blue sky.

4. Allow the children to decorate paper butterfly or egg shapes with sponge painting, crayons, glitter, sequins, ribbon, colored crushed egg shells, foil, macaroni, crayons, paper confetti, etc.

5. Cut out various Easter shapes such as bunnies, chicks, baskets, eggs, butterflies, and crosses from various colors of construction paper or wallpaper. Give the children an egg-shaped piece of paper and allow them to glue the shapes on any way they wish (collage form).

6. Let the children glue cotton balls to a lamb shape to make its soft coat.

7. Plant seeds in paper or styrofoam cups and talk about the things the seeds will need to grow. Choose seeds that will germinate quickly.

A good way to celebrate Easter in your class is to have a party. Set a table with a tablecloth and flowers and decorate the room with pastel-colored balloons and crepe paper. Ask parents to donate "springy" looking plates, napkins and cups. A good treat to have is cookies cut out in Easter shapes such as bunnies, chicks, crosses, baskets, etc., iced in pastel colors. One of the moms may be glad to make these for you. If your facilities permit, ask the parents to join you for the party. Make your celebration truly festive so that the children realize that Easter is very special. In a large parish where I was in charge of the preschool/kindergarten program on Sunday, our Easter party was the biggest party of the year. All ninety children gathered in the gym for a Bible enthronement service, filmstrip or play, songs, fingerplays and snacks. It was wonderful—and the children knew that something special was going on!

Parents of your children may be wondering how to celebrate Easter with their little ones (besides providing new clothes and chocolate Easter bunnies). It is important that you share your class activities with them so that they are able to continue the appropriate religious focus at home. You could send a letter home like the one below following your class presentation on Easter.

Dear Parents:

We have been speaking about spring and new life to your children in class to prepare them to celebrate the great feast of Easter. We all know that in the spring, new life appears all around us and plants and trees begin to bud and sprout. More changes take place, however, that are unseen. The frozen water in the ground thaws and the roots of trees and plants grow stronger and longer to partake of the life-giving water. The trunks, stems, and branches all grow thicker and the whole plant gains strength in this season of new life. What a beautiful analogy to Lent and Easter! We discover the stagnant and "dead" parts of our lives and reach to the resurrected Lord, the "Living Water," for strengthening and growth. Each Lent and Easter become seasons of "new life" for us, for renewed growth and reaffirmed faith in Jesus.

Of course, our little ones are not able to grasp these spiritual mysteries of the death and resurrection of Jesus, but they are able to appreciate the beauty and wonder of the new life in spring all around them. They are especially enthralled by the story of the homely little caterpillar, who by some marvelous and mysterious transformation, turns into a beautiful butterfly. They are amazed by the wonder of a "dead" looking seed being planted in the ground and mysteriously sprouting to new life. How good God is! For adults, all of these mysteries point to and are perfected in the death (as in the cocoon and the seed) and new life (the butterfly and the plant) of Jesus. As the childen grow and mature, they will be able to relate to these great mysteries because of their appreciation of the natural wonders around them.

Our role as parents is to "become as children" and delight in the natural wonders of spring with our little ones. We need to celebrate these wonders with our children as special gifts of Gód. Ultimately, we need to live as examples of the joy and happiness we find in this renewed life in Jesus. Here are some activities that you can do with your little one to emphasize "new life in spring:"

1. Go for a "new life" walk with your child and look for signs of spring. If possible, bring some "treasures" home. Place these on a prayer table or in a prominent spot so that you can be reminded to thank God for spring.

2. Plant some seeds with your child. (Choose seeds that germinate quickly!) Talk about the seeds; discuss how they look dry and dead. Then talk about the things that the seeds need to grow and how God's power makes the seeds grow into new life.

3. Color Easter eggs with your child or have an Easter egg hunt. Talk about how some animals hatch from eggs (chicks, birds, snakes, turtles, etc.) and how God gives us new life through eggs.

4. Try to capture a butterfly for your child (gently please!) and put it into a glass jar for a short time so that they can see it up close. Be sure to let the butterfly go after your child has observed it.

CELEBRATING PENTECOST

"When the time for Pentecost was fulfilled, they were all in one place together. And suddenly there came from the sky a noise like a strong driving wind, and it filled the house in which they were. And they were all filled with the Holy Spirit." Acts 2: 1-2, 4

The feast of Pentecost is indeed one of our great feasts: it marks the birth of the redemptive work of the church. By receiving the wisdom, courage and strength of the Spirit, the apostles were finally ready to begin the work of the proclamation of the kingdom. And to this day, it is through the working of the Spirit that the church continues to preach the Good News of Jesus Christ.

Our little ones, however, are not able to understand or relate to the action of the Spirit in our faith lives. Just the mention of the word "spirit" may conjure up many images in the minds of the children that we would not choose to express the loving care of the Holy Spirit! Two themes which the children are able to relate to and understand can be used to celebrate the feast of Pentecost with them: a presentation on air, and a birthday party for the church. Here are some ideas that you can use to incorporate these themes into your class:

1. Decorate your classroom with balloons. Make sure you have enough balloons so that each of the children can take one home when class is over.

2. You could have a small fan with streamers attached

blowing and also have a kite displayed or hanging somewhere in the room.

3. If you have any pictures of wind "working" (e.g., sailboats, clothes drying on a line, kites flying, trees blowing, etc.), they could be displayed.

4. Talk to the children about air and wind. You could blow up a balloon for them or use a pinwheel to begin your discussion. "What is it that makes the balloon get big and makes the pinwheel move?" Talk about the many ways children experience air and wind. Some items and experiences you can use to explain how air and wind work are whistles, musical instruments (harmonicas and horns), cool breezes on a hot day, clouds floating by, flying kites, sailboats, having their hats blown off, blowing out birthday candles, flags waving, car or bicycle tires, bubbles, storms, (blowing rain or snow), etc. Your discussion will be enhanced if you are able to have some of the objects you are discussing with you in class.

The children can encounter air in your class in several ways. If it is a nice day, take the children outside and let them blow bubbles. Talk about how the children use air to make the bubbles. Give the children crepe paper streamers or scarves and let them "dance" while making the streamers move through the air. Music which changes tempo would be good to use: encourage the children to listen so they'll know whether to be a "strong wind" or a "gentle breeze." You can also put sand (or confetti paper, rice, cereal, etc.) in an appropriate container and let the children gently blow designs in it using straws. Or, the children could blow bubbles in a pan of water using straws.

When the children are quiet again, ask them to watch you breathe (breathe deeply!). Let them listen to and watch themselves breathe. Talk about how we need air to live and that God made our bodies so perfect that they remember to breathe on their own. Tell the children to hold their hands in front of their mouths and blow on them. That way, they'll be able to feel the air that helps them to live. Talk about other things that need air to live, such as plants and animals. Tell the children how good God is to have given us the gift of air, and explain all the wonderful things it does for us. Pray with the children, thanking God for this wonderful gift. You may want to sing the following song as a prayer:

(Tune: Frere Jacques)
Thank you, God, for the air
Strong, strong wind, gentle breeze.
And the air we breathe, keeping us alive,
Thank you, God; we love you!

There are several different crafts that the children could do to accompany this lesson:

1. Using a sheet of blue construction paper, allow the children to make clouds by gluing cotton balls on the paper. Have the children pull the cotton apart a little to look "fluffy."

2. Have the children make pinwheels. Directions for these can be found in craft books or in the library.

3. Show the children how to make kites. Glue four paint stirrers together in the shape of a kite. Allow the children to decorate kite-shaped pieces of paper and glue them to the frame. Make tails out of ribbon, crepe paper or yarn. Or, simply paste kite-shaped pieces of paper on construction paper; the children can then decorate the kites and add tails.

4. Glue a piece of string or yarn between two "poles" on a piece of construction paper. Have the children cut from catalogues (or select pre-cut) pictures of clothes and hang (glue) their "laundry" on the line to dry in the wind.

5. Have the children fold and make paper fans. They can decorate them before they are folded.

Depending on your facilities and the number of children in your program, there are several ways to hold a birthday party for the church. You could plan to have a special program such as a puppet show, movie, a children's singing group, theatre troupe etc. and invite the parents to view the program with their children. Be sure to include a birthday cake complete with candles to be blown out after you sing "Happy Birthday!" Balloons for decorations and birthday party hats will add to the party atmosphere.

Explain to the children why you are having a birthday party, as some may be confused by Jesus' birthday celebration at Christmas. You may offer a simple explanation similar to the following: "Do you know whose birthday it is? Today we are having a birthday party for our church! This day is like the birthday of our country that we celebrate on the Fourth of July. Do you remember what we do on the Fourth of July? We have picnics, parades and sometimes even fireworks! We won't have any fireworks today for our church's birthday party, but we are going to have (here you may explain your program) to help us celebrate. This party is our way of saying "thank you" to God for giving us our church family." In planning this party, be sure to include some type of refreshments, be it cake, cookies, or donut holes, and drinks. There is nothing like food to complete a celebration!

If you are not able to secure a program, you may include a birthday party celebration as part of your class. Set a table with a special birthday tablecloth, have a cake with candles, party hats, balloons, etc. You may want to invite parents to share in this part of your class. Be sure to explain to them whose birthday it is!

Below is a sample of a parent letter that could be sent home after your class on air:

Dear Parents:
Today in our class we discussed the gift of air that God gives us. We talked about the many things air and wind help us "do," such as fly kites, dry clothes, sail

boats, play certain instruments, blow up balloons, make pinwheels work, etc. We also talked about how important air is because we need it to live. We watched and listened to ourselves breathe and talked about how animals and plants need air to live, too.

This lesson on air was presented as a way to celebrate the feast of Pentecost with your child. The children are too young to understand the workings of the Holy Spirit in our church, but can understand the power and necessity of air and wind, which is a great symbol of the descent of the Holy Spirit. While they were not taught this symbolism, they were introduced to the many facets of this wonderful gift of God. Listed below are some activities that you can do with your children to increase their thankfulness (and yours!) for the gift of air:

1. (Here you may list any of the craft activities that you did not do in your class.)

2. Fly a kite with your children, reminding them how special the gift of air is.

3. On a sunny, windy day, go outside with your children and watch the shadows the trees make as the wind blows through them.

CELEBRATING MARY

"I am the servant of the Lord. Let it be done to me as you say."
Luke 1:38

May is traditionally the month devoted to Mary. She remains important in the lives of Christians all year, however, as an example of how we can be open to the will of God. She remained faithful to his plan for her and was subjected to many trials and sufferings. Even though she was the mother of Jesus, things were not easy for her.

Mary was very young and probably frightened when she agreed to be the mother of Jesus. Even after she said yes, her life was not a peaceful one. She came from a very small town and when news of her pregnancy became known, tongues surely wagged. Her baby was born in a stable in a strange town, after a very long journey on a donkey. She and Joseph were forced to flee to Egypt shortly after Jesus was born—they were political refugees of a sort. Finally, they were able to return home, where we assume that their life resumed some normalcy.

If any of us have experienced having lost a child, we know how frantic Mary was when Jesus was lost for three days in Jerusalem. Can you imagine how she must have felt? God had entrusted her with his son and she had lost him! When he was found, Mary was confronted with the rebelliousness of an adolescent. Surely she must have wondered what God held in store for her and for Jesus. She became a widow at a relatively young age and was forced to spend the time alone when Jesus was preaching. She also endured his suffering and death alone, and there is no greater pain than to bury one's child.

We need to concentrate on these very human facts of Mary's life to realize that she was human and probably endured much more than any of us ever will. But through it all, she remained constantly faithful to God, knowing that he would work things out in his own way and in his own time. And he did.

Of course, we cannot teach these truths to our little ones just yet. In our preschool/kindergarten classes, we encourage the children to think about Mary in relation to their own mothers. This is one lesson in which the children's life experiences will be easy to draw upon; all of the children are familiar with mothers (or a mother figure) and will eagerly join in a discussion about them. Our aim in this lesson is to begin to instill a sense of love and devotion to Mary by relating her to the children's own mothers. Drawing upon the love they have for their own mothers, they can be shown how special Mary was to Jesus and how special she should be to us, too.

We first want to talk to children about their mothers. An easy way to do this is to have some pictures of moms doing things with their children. Pictures depicting moms cooking, cleaning, washing clothes, reading stories, taking a walk, playing, or taking care of a sick child could be used to discuss all the ways moms love them. If you do not have good pictures to use, try using a flannel board and symbols for various activities moms do. For example, a broom, story book, an iron, a stove, a thermometer, etc., could be used to elicit discussion. You can draw these items or cut pictures from coloring books, magazines or catalogues. There are, of course, many stories about mothers available in the library that also could be used. Tell the children it's not always easy to be a mommy, but our moms love us so much and want to help us and be with us. Our moms know that God picked them especially for us, to be our mothers, and they are happy to do what God wants. Ask the children to tell you something special about their mothers and how their moms take care of them and love them. They will be eager to participate!

You may want to sing the following song to reinforce your discussion on mothers:

(Tune: Here We Go 'Round the Mulberry Bush—use appropriate actions)
1. This is the way Mom washes the clothes,
   washes the clothes, washes the clothes.
   This is the way Mom washes the clothes.
   My Mom is good to me.
2. This is the way Mom cooks the meal, etc.
3. This is the way Mom sweeps the floor, etc.

4. This is the way we read a story, etc.
5. This is the way we take a walk, etc.

Let the children suggest additional verses and actions for the song.

Try to find a good picture of Mary and Jesus together. Coloring books are a good source for these pictures. Show the children the picture and talk about Mary. Ask the children if they know their mom's first name. Tell them that Jesus' mother had a first name too, and it was ... (see if they are able to tell you). Tell them that Mary did the same things for Jesus that their moms do for them. She taught him to walk and talk, she washed his clothes and cooked his meals, she helped him if he fell down and hurt his knee, etc. It was not always easy for Mary to be Jesus' mother, but she knew God chose her to be Jesus' mother and she was happy to do what God wanted. Jesus loved his mother very much, just like you love your mom. Jesus and his mother are in heaven now, and Jesus wants us to love his mother, too. He told us that she could be our mother, so we have two special mothers; our moms at our house and Jesus' mother in heaven. We can talk to Mary and thank her for taking such good care of Jesus and ask her to watch over us, too. We can say a little prayer like this:

> Dear Mary, thank you for being Jesus' mother and for being our mother, too. Watch over us and help us to do good things like you taught Jesus to do. We love you. Watch over our moms at home, too, and help them when their jobs are hard. Amen.

The children could also sing the following song about Mary:

(Tune: Mary Had a Little Lamb)
1. Jesus had a special Mom, special Mom, special Mom, Jesus had a special Mom, and her name was Mary.

2. Mary helped him grow and learn, grow and learn, grow and learn,
   Mary helped him grow and learn, to do the right things.
3. Mary is our Mom too, our Mom too, our Mom too,
   Mary is our Mom too, and we love her so.
4. Mary helps us to be good, to be good, to be good,
   Mary helps us to be good, just like she helped Jesus.

There are several craft ideas that you could use for this lesson to reinforce your ideas about mothers and Mary.

1. Make a hand print of each child (trace or print with paint) and have the children draw colorful flowers on the fingertips (as a handful of flowers for their moms!). Or they could use the hand print as a flower and add stems, leaves, more petals, etc.

2. Give the children a piece of construction paper with the outline of a flower on it. Fill the inside of the flower by spreading with glue. Using dry colored breakfast cereal, have the children fill in the outline of the flower.

3. Let the children weave paper strips into a placemat or design. Explain that Mary used to weave cloth to make clothes for Jesus. Be sure to use contrasting colors for the strips so that the children can see what they are doing.

4. If your facilities permit, make bread with the children. Perhaps you might bring the dough already mixed and let the children knead it. Explain that Mary used to make bread for Jesus to eat. (Use a "eucharistic bread" recipe and make the loaves round and flat, as Mary probably did.)

5. Have the children make flowers to give to their moms. There are many ways to do this. Have the children choose pre-cut pictures of flowers (seed catalogues are good sources for these pictures) and glue them onto pre-drawn stems. Let them add leaves and scenery if they wish. Small crumpled pieces of tissue paper, colored miniature marshmallows, or

colored cereal can be glued inside outlines of flowers. Use nut cups or cupcake papers and glue them to predrawn stems.

6. "Treasure boxes" using fast food styrofoam sandwich containers make a nice gift for mother. Decorate them using macaroni, dried beans, peas, beads, buttons, etc. These gifts could be sprayed with paint by the teacher when the children are finished.

As the children learn that Jesus' mother was just like their moms, they will begin to know and love Mary. With this knowledge and love, they can later come to honor her as a woman who faithfully lived in total acceptance of God's will and to follow her example. Mary is a perfect model for Christain behavior because she totally trusted in God's plan no matter how difficult life became. It is wise then to remind the parents of this fact and encourage them to follow her example and to talk about Mary to their little ones. You may want to send a letter home such as the one that follows.

Dear Parents:
(I suggest using the four introductory paragraphs of this section on Mary to begin your letter to parents, beginning with "May is traditionally" and ending with "and he did." You could then add the following.)

Our little ones cannot understand these truths just yet, but they can understand that Jesus had a mother just like they do. In our class on Mary, we encouraged the children to think about Mary in relation to their own mothers. We talked about what their moms do for them and what Jesus' mother must have done for him. Even though the era in which Jesus and Mary lived was very different from ours, Mary cooked, cleaned, washed clothes, played with and comforted Jesus just as mothers do today. We told them that it was not always easy for Mary to be Jesus' mother, but she knew that was what God wanted her to do. We also told the children how special Mary is to Jesus and that he wants her to be our mother, too. She is with Jesus in heaven now, but she watches over us and helps us to do good things just like she taught Jesus to do.

As parents, we have a twofold job. We need to pattern our lives after Mary, in the spirit of her total acceptance of God's presence and will in her life. We also need to encourage our little ones to look upon Mary as Jesus' mother who took care of him on earth and as their special mother in heaven. Following are some things you can do with your child to "celebrate Mary."

1. Choose a picture of Mary for your child to have. If Mary is to be their special mother in heaven, they may want a picture to look at. Choose a picture from a religious goods store, coloring book, or story book. Be sure the picture is one that will appeal to your little one.

2. Bake bread with your child at home, allowing them to knead it and help form the loaves. Be sure to remind them that Mary made all the bread for Jesus because they didn't have any stores where they could buy it.

3. For mothers: Reflect on your role as a mother. Do you give selflessly in true love or do you expect things in return ("After all I've done for you!")?

CELEBRATING SAINTS

"You are my friends. It was not you who chose me, it was I who chose you to go forth and bear fruit." John 15:14, 16

Saints are those friends of God who have indeed borne fruit in the holy and virtuous lives they have led. They are men and women whose example spurs us on to do great things in the Lord. Their accomplishments and rewards also give us hope that one day we, too, will find eternal life with the Father as Jesus promised by following his way of life. We venerate the saints and ask them to pray for us as members of our church who have already attained what is promised to those who believe and act.

In speaking of saints as friends of God to our little ones, we must first make sure that they understand what a friend is. Three-, four-, and five-year-olds are just beginning to make friends and to realize that other people do exist besides themselves. So in talking about the saints, it is a good idea to begin with a lesson on friends. (There is related material to this section on friends in the lesson on Lent.)

By presenting a story about friends, you can begin to instill in the children some of the attitudes that friends have toward each other. Choose a book or story from the library that will show kindness, love, and sharing among friends. Your stories do not have to be limited to "human" friends. Sesame Street friends and animal friends will help the children understand friendship using characters that they are familiar with. Talk to the children about friends that they have and how they show love for each other. Ask them what they do with their friends, and be sure to relate some experiences about your friendships with people (how you have helped or have been helped by your friends).

Be sure to tell the children that their friends are special gifts from God. God gives us friends so that we are not lonely and so that we can share his love with them. Following are two songs that you can use to help the children understand what you have been telling them about friends.

(Tune: Mary Had a Little Lamb)
Friends are special gifts from God, gifts from God,
   gifts from God,

Friends are special gifts from God.
We thank God for our friends.

(Tune: Here We Go 'Round the Mulberry Bush)
1. This is the way we love our friends,
   love our friends, love our friends,
   This is the way we love our friends
   And show our love for God.
2. This is the way we help our friends...
   And pick up all the toys.
3. This is the way we're kind to friends...
   and share our snacks with them.

As you are discussing friends, tell the children about the special friends of God, the saints. When we say "saint," we usually think of a very good person who has died and is now living in heaven with God. They did special things to help other people and to share God's love with them. Tell the children the stories of one or two saints. You will want to choose stories of saints that the children can realistically imitate (no martyrs or visionaries at this point!). St. Joseph is a good choice. All the children are familiar with what a father is and will understand all the special things Joseph did (took care of Jesus and Mary, worked in the carpenter shop, etc.) that showed how much he loved God. St. Francis, with his love of animals and creation, is another good choice. Perhaps you could tell the children the following story about Francis:

> St. Francis is a saint who lived a long time ago. He loved all the good things that God made in the world; he loved the sun, the moon, the stars, the fire, the wind, and the water. He knew God made all these things because God loves us so much and he even wrote a song to thank God for all these gifts. St. Francis especially loved animals and sometimes he talked to

them and told them how much God loved them too. Here is a little story about St. Francis and the birds.

One day, St. Francis was trying to teach some people about God and Jesus and the people did not want to listen to him. This made St. Francis very sad and he went into the woods for a walk. He saw the birds in the trees and decided that since the people didn't want to listen, he would tell the birds how much God loved them. The birds stopped their chirping and listened to St. Francis. When he was done, the birds started singing a beautiful song to thank St. Francis for telling them how much God loved them. The things St. Francis did always remind us to be especially thankful to God for all the animals he has given us.

This story about St. Francis could lead into a discussion about animals and pets and how the children can take good care of God's creatures that he gives us.

Several other saints whose stories you could use with the children are St. Nicholas, St. Patrick, St. Elizabeth of Hungary, and St. John Bosco. The paperback series "Book of Saints" by Rev. Lovasik, SVD (Catholic Book Publishing Co. New York, 1982) has some good quality pictures of these saints that you can use. Emphasize the good deeds that the saints performed and encourage the children to do the same. It is important to realize that a lesson on friends and saints with preschool and kindergarten-age children must deal with concrete facts and experiences. At this age, they are not able to deal with abstract signs or principles. So keep your discussion of the saints very simple and concrete. Dwell on the good works performed and not on miracles, appearances and visions, and martyrdom.

Tell the children that they, too, are special friends of God and can do things to show how much they love God. Talk about some ways that they can show God's love and be like the saints (e.g., sharing toys and snacks; donating canned goods to the poor and baking cookies for the elderly; speaking kindly to one another; helping each other; being kind to and taking care of their pets; taking care of nature by picking up papers; etc.). Pray with the children using the following prayer or song:

> Dear God, thank you for helping the saints do good things so that they could show us how to be like you. Please help us to be kind and helpful like your saints and to show your love to everyone. Amen.
>
> *(Tune: Mary Had a Little Lamb)*
> 1. Saints are special friends of God, friends of God, friends of God.
>   Saints are special friends of God
>   who showed us how to live.
> 2. We will try to be like them,
>   be like them, be like them.
>   We will try to be like them
>   and show your love to all.
> 3. Thank you, God, for all the saints,
>   all the saints, all the saints.
>   Thank you, God, for all the saints,
>   your very special friends.

There are several craft ideas that could emphasize the idea of either friends or saints:

1. Pass out four paper leaves to each child to be colored or decorated in any way each chooses. When they are finished, have them trade two or three leaves with others in the class. Now each child has four leaves for his or her own "friendship tree." Have the children paste their leaves on a piece of construction paper which has the outline of a tree on it. (Each child will have his or her own tree.)

2. Have each child choose a favorite-colored crayon. Give

every child a piece of drawing paper and make sure their names are on it. Have the children begin drawing whatever they like and when a bell rings (after about a minute) have the children pass their paper to the next child to continue the drawing. Continue until the children have their own papers back. (If you have a large group of children, split the class into two groups for this activity.) Comment on how all of our friends in class helped color our paper, our "sharing picture."

3. With four- and five-year-olds, have two children work on a picture together, creating a "partner picture." In the picture, have the children show a way they could be like a saint (or a good friend). These pictures should be displayed for the parents, so that there are no arguments over who takes the picture home!

4. Do a craft or project related to the saint whose story you have told, such as: have the children draw or find pictures of tools (catalogues) that St. Joseph would have used in his carpenter shop or something that he would have made. Have the children glue feathers or pieces of yarn onto bird shapes to remind them of St. Francis. Let the children draw or glue pictures of roses (from a seed catalogue) onto an apron, drawn on a piece of construction paper, to help them remember the story of St. Elizabeth.

Our appreciation of the saints has been misunderstood over the years by many because of the sometimes erroneous "adoration" that has been given them. It would be wise to communicate with the parents about the saints, and in doing so, enable them to relate to these great and special friends of God. Perhaps you could send a letter to the parents such as the following:

Dear Parents:
Today we talked about friends and about the special friends of God, the saints. We were careful to choose

stories about saints that the children could understand and imitate in their own ways. It is important to keep these stories very simple and concrete for the little ones and avoid stories of martyrs, visionaries, and miracle workers. They will come to understand these aspects of sainthood at a later time in their development. At this time, they need to know that the saints were special friends of God who showed his love to all the people they met. They were kind and helpful, and we want to be like them and show God's love, too.

As adults, we must remember that the saints are not "gods," but humans who have passed into eternal life, as Jesus has promised. They offer us hope that this life is indeed attainable and spur us on to a greater participation in the kind of life that we are charged to live as Christians. We must remember that the saints are still members of our church community too those who have attained their goals, and that we are able to ask them to pray for us just as we ask those members of the church on earth to pray for us. It is through this intercessory power that they are able to help us as living members of our church community.

Probably the best way to teach your children about the saints is to celebrate them! Choose saints whose lives are easily understood by the children and plan ways to celebrate their feasts at home. Here are some suggestions for doing so. Be sure to briefly explain to your children why you are celebrating!

1. St. Patrick's Day (March 17) Decorate your home or table with shamrocks and green napkins, serve green jello, green eggs (!), cupcakes with green icing, etc.

2. St. Joseph's Day (March 19) Make this a special day for dad (or an uncle or grandfather) in honor of St. Joseph. Cook dad's favorite meal, have your children help with a dessert and help your child make a card for dad, thanking him for all the things he does for the family (like St. Joseph did for his family).

3. St. Francis' Feast Day (October 4) Make this a day to celebrate animals and pets. Visit a pet shop or a zoo, serve "rabbit food" (salad) for dinner, make animal-shaped cookies with your children, give the dog a bath!

4. St. Elizabeth of Hungary (November 17) or St. Vincent de Paul (September 27) Make bread or rolls with your children and take them to someone who is house-bound. Shop for some canned goods for a food pantry. Visit someone who is ill or in a nursing home and help your children make a card or small favor to take along.

5. St. Nicholas Day (December 6) Fill stockings or shoes with treats for your child. Allow them to make paper stockings and tape a treat, such as a candy cane, to it. Deliver the stocking to a friend, elderly person or shut-in.

CELEBRATING THANKSGIVING

"Come and see the works of God, his tremendous deeds among us. Bless our God, you peoples, loudly sound his praises."

Psalm 66: 5, 8

It is always good to give thanks to the Lord for all the wonderful gifts he has given us, and Thanksgiving gives us the opportunity to do that in a special way. Giving thanks is one thing that many people neglect in their prayer lives; it seems we spend more time in supplication and petition! Thanksgiving gives us the opportunity to stop and reflect on the good things that God has given us and to express our thanks and praise. Our lives should be filled with thanks and praise, not only for the material things we have received but for the love and friendship that God has chosen to share with us.

It is an awesome thought when we reflect on it. Our God cares for us and loves each of us personally and has showered us with many gifts and talents. The feast of Thanksgiving originated because the Pilgrims were thankful for survival in that first year in the New World. And that survival came about with much help from their friends, the Indians (Native Americans). Many of the gifts we have received have come through others, too, and we also have had the opportunity to share the wealth of God's love through the use of the gifts we have been given. The feast of Thanksgiving is many-faceted, and should serve as a springboard for daily reflection, praise, and thanks for our gifts.

Giving thanks is a concept that our little ones can readily understand. They are able to experience the gifts that God has bestowed on them and it is our job to make them aware of these gifts and who has given them. There are several ways that you can accomplish this. Obtain some books and pictures about Thanksgiving that the children can look at before class while everyone is arriving. These pictures should depict more than the traditional Thanksgiving (Pilgrims, Native Americans, turkeys, etc.), although they should be included. Pictures of things the children are thankful for (ie, families, friends, animals, sun, snow, etc.), pictures of people sharing (farmers, grocers, community helpers, etc.) should also be among your pictures.

Call the children together and talk about Thanksgiving, using the pictures you have been looking at. You may want to present a very simple version of the first Thanksgiving using a flannel board or large pictures. Tell the story in your own words; this is one you know well! Be sure to keep it simple, as the children will not easily understand the political reasons for the pilgrims coming to America or the need for religious freedom. Explain to the children why we celebrate Thanksgiving by saying that every year we take time to remind ourselves to thank God for all of his gifts to us. This is why we always have a big dinner, a "feast" with our families like the Pilgrims and Native Americans did, to celebrate Thanksgiving. Use the pictures and books the children have been looking at to remind them about all of God's gifts. Perhaps each child can pick a picture of something he or she is especially grateful for and tell the class about it. Be sure that you tell the children what you are grateful for, too!

It is also important to discuss that God wants us to share our gifts with other people, too; this is one of the reasons he gave them to us. No matter how poor we are, there always seems to be someone who is worse off—and the children need to begin to understand that it's our duty, our "job" as Christians, to take care of those less fortunate. You can simply explain that there are many people in the world—and even in your own city or town—who do not have enough to eat or a place to live. Explain how many people have started places where people can come to get food to eat and to take home to their families. We can help by giving food or money to these places. We can help find clothes for poor people by giving them the clothes that don't fit us anymore or the ones we don't need. You could show the children some canned food and perhaps some baby clothes (clothes they would have grown out of!) and encourage them to ask their parents to help poor people.

One nice way to reinforce this concept of giving thanks and sharing is to have each child bring in a can of food (you will need to send a note home to parents the week before). You can plan a very simple prayer service which includes a procession of all the children during which they come forward and place their food in a basket or box. The following are prayers and songs that you can use for this prayer service:

Dear God, you have given us many gifts and we want to say thank you for them. Thank you for our families and our friends, our houses and the food that we have, and the clothes that we wear. Please help us to share our gifts with those who do not have as much as we do. Amen.

(Tune: Frere Jacques)
We are thankful, we are thankful
to our God, to our God.
He has given good things
To us and to our families.
Thank you, God, we love you!

(Tune: Twinkle, Twinkle, Little Star)
We are thankful for good things,
God has sent and so we sing.
Food and families, friends and snow,
Flowers, trees, and things that grow.
Thank you, God, for all your care,
Help us now to love and share.

There are many craft ideas that you could use with a lesson on Thanksgiving. Try one of the following.

1. Make "thankful" turkeys. The children can color the body of a turkey and pick different colored paper feathers for the tail. The children can then tell what they are thankful for and you and your helper could write it on the feathers, which are then glued on the turkey. (You could also have the "gifts" already printed on the feathers, ie., food, family, friends, animals, etc.). Or, the children could spread their fingers on a sheet of paper and trace around their hand to make the body of a turkey. The gifts could be printed on the feathers (fingers) and then colored.

2. Let the children make a "thankful collage." Cut pictures of food, homes, clothing, toys, etc., from magazines or

catalogues and allow the children to choose the things they're thankful for. Glue the pictures on construction paper or on a large pre-cut form of a turkey.

3. Have pre-cut pictures of different kinds of food. Label the rim of a paper plate with the words, "We thank God for food." Let the children pick the foods they like best and paste on the plate.

4. Make turkey shapes from sponges using a cookie cutter and allow the children to decorate placemats by dipping sponges in tempera paint. The children could "fringe" the edges by snipping with scissors.

5. Ask the parents to supply some turkey-shaped cookies and some canned frosting and let the children ice and decorate the cookies in class. Use these for a snack or let the children take them home and share them.

One way to impress upon the children the importance of Thanksgiving is to celebrate it in the classroom! Snack time can be very special for this class. Set the table with a cloth and flowers, using festive napkins, cups, and plates. An easy celebration and one that emphasizes sharing nicely is making a fruit salad. The week before your Thanksgiving class, send notes home with the children asking the parents to send a specific amount of fruit with the children. They may be asked to supply the plates, cups, napkins, and a drink, too.

Ideally, the children should be able to wash, peel, and slice the fruit themselves to really share in making the fruit salad. Depending on your facilities and the number of children in your class, however, this may not be possible. Instead, the children may gather around the teacher and watch as she prepares each child's fruit for the salad. This works equally well. Be sure to comment on who brought the fruit and thank them for sharing it with the class. Comment also on how different each fruit is, how good it smells and how good God is for making so many different kinds of fruit for us. Gather the children around the table and pray, thanking God for the fruit and supplies, for the children who brought them and for any other gifts you wish to mention. You may say this prayer in the form of a litany, with the children responding, "Thank you, God," after each gift you mention. (You may want to say this litany-type prayer as you are preparing the fruit, thanking God for the fruit and for the child who brought it as you "go along.") If your facilities permit, you may want to ask parents to join in this Thanksgiving feast. This is a nice way to involve the parents in your activities, and the children love to have their parents come to class!

By actually involving the children in a Thanksgiving celebration that they can share in and prepare, they are able to understand the true meaning of Thanksgiving a little bit better: to give thanks to our heavenly Father for all the gifts and to share those gifts in whatever way they are able.

You will need to send a note home the week before your class. What you write will depend on what activities you are planning. You will need to ask for a specific amount of fruit (usually one piece is enough, such as one apple, one banana, one pear, etc.), a nonperishable food item for your food collection, and an invitation for the parents to attend the "feast." The following letter could be sent home after your class on Thanksgiving:

> Dear Parents:
> Today we celebrated the feast of Thanksgiving with your children. We talked about all the good gifts that God has given us, such as families, food, friends, pets, clothes, houses, etc. and we thanked God for these gifts in prayer. We also talked about sharing our gifts with those who have less than we do and the different ways that we can do this, i.e., contributions to food pantries, clothing drives, etc.

Your role in developing an attitude of thankfulness and satisfaction in your children is most important! We should be thankful for our blessings all of the time and not just at Thanksgiving. It is necessary to thank God daily and to share what we have. Jesus' commands in the gospels to be thankful, to feed the hungry and help the poor are very explicit and not to be ignored. We teach our children to follow these commands of Jesus by our example, by our thankfulness and willingness to share what we have. We need to be satisfied with what we have and not make the acquisition of material goods the main purpose of our lives. This is very difficult to do in our consumer-oriented culture, but it is the Christian way to live. Following are some suggestions for you to use at home to help develop an attitude of thankfulness and generosity in your children:

1. Say grace at meals and allow your children to participate by either saying grace or allowing them to add something special they are thankful for. Spontaneous, "homemade" prayers are best!

2. Take your children shopping and allow them to help choose some canned goods for a local food pantry. Help them to make good choices of healthy food.

3. Go through your clothes and give away things that you don't need or wear any more. Let your children go through some baby clothes and give away items that do not fit any more.

4. Limit the amount of television your children view. Many of the wants and "needs" of children are derived from television advertising of toys, especially prior to Christmas. This type of advertising makes children (and adults) feel dissatisfied with what they have and always want more. Turn off the television and read or play a game with your children; you'll all be better off for it!

APPENDIX

The following section provides some additional information for planning simple prayer services that can be used with three-, four-, and five-year-olds. Prayer services allow the children to become familiar with community song and prayer, processions and ceremony. They will recognize all these elements in the liturgy as their understanding of the Mass and our community celebrations matures.

The format for the prayer service is outlined in Chapter 3, in the section, "Teachers." The following "samples" could be used in a religious education preschool or kindergarten class in the spring, celebrating St. Joseph and fathers, Lent and Easter. These examples will encourage you to write your own!

A list of paraphrased Bible verses that could be used in planning a prayer service or litany prayer has also been included. Following this is a listing of some audio visual resources that would be useful in presenting the lessons on the church and celebrating the liturgical year. Most of the resources listed here are filmstrips, as they are short enough to accomodate the young child's attention span.

PRAYER SERVICES FOR YOUNG CHILDREN

Celebrating St. Joseph and Fathers

Opening Song *(Tune: Frere Jacques):*
We are coming to the table.
Gather 'round, gather 'round
listening to God's word, listening to God's word.
We love him, we love him.

Prayer: Dear God, St Joseph was a special father to Jesus when he lived on earth. Jesus loved him very much. Please help us to love and help our own fathers just like Jesus did.

Story: Joseph was worried about being Jesus' father. He knew Jesus would be a very special boy because he was God's son. God told Joseph not to worry because Joseph was a good man and would be the best father for Jesus. Joseph decided to be Jesus' father and taught him to be a carpenter and make things out of wood just like he did (based on Matt. 1:18-24).

Litany: Response: We love you, God!
Thank you, God, for St. Joseph, who was such a good father to Jesus and taught him many things.
Thank you, God, for my own father, who loves me and teaches me many things, too.
Thank you, God, for all the nice things my father does for me and let me be a good helper to him, too.

Closing Song *(Tune: Twinkle, Twinkle, Little Star):*
Joseph made things out of wood.
He showed Jesus all he could.
Gave him food and clothes and love,
showed him sun and stars above.
Played with him and hugged him tight
He loved Jesus day and night.

Celebrating New Life in Spring (Easter)

Opening Song (See page 105)

Prayer: Dear God, we thank you and your son Jesus for the new life we see all around us in the spring. We especially thank you for lettting the plants start to grow again and poke out of the dirt. Everything is so pretty and green! You are so good to us!

Story: One day Jesus was telling his friends how much God loved them. He told them about a man who went into his garden and planted some seeds. He watered them and went home to eat his supper and go to bed. Every day he went to work and came home and checked the garden. Finally the seeds started to poke out of the ground and grow all by themselves! The man didn't really know how it happened. Jesus told his friends that God makes the seeds grow for us. God loves us so much and wants us to have pretty flowers and vegetables, so God makes the seeds grow (based on Mark 4:26-29).

> **Litany:** Response: We thank you, God, for new life!
> For all the new little plants that are starting to grow
> For all the butterflies that will be coming out of their cocoons
> For all the new baby lambs and chicks
> For all the beautiful flowers.
>
> **Closing Song** *(Tune: Frere Jacques):*
> Spring is new life, spring is new life.
> Winter's gone, winter's gone.
> Baby chicks are peeping, caterpillars creeping.
> Spring is here, thank you, God.

We Celebrate Lent

Opening Song (See page 105)

Prayer: Dear God, this is a special time of year when people try to live like Jesus did and do kind things. Help us to be more like Jesus was.

Story: Once when Jesus was eating a special meal with his friends, He said to them: "I will show you the way to live, to be kind and helpful, and you will have a good life and be happy" (based on John 14:6).

Litany: Response: Jesus, we will try to be just like you.
Help us to show our love for our mom and dad by helping them at home
Help us to always treat our friends nicely, and share our toys
Help us to always listen to our teacher and do what she tells us to do
Help us to be kind to people who are sick or lonely or poor

Closing Song *(Tune: Ten Little Indians):*
I will be a loving child, I will be a helping child
I will be a friendly child, I will live like Jesus did.

PARAPHRASED BIBLE VERSES
Jesus loves little children. (Mk. 10:13-16)
Share your food with hungry people. (Is. 58:7)
God gave us seeds. (Gen. 1:25)
God is love. (1 Jn. 4:8)
God gave us the earth (water, light). (Gen. 1:10)
Jesus said, "You are my friends." (Jn. 15:15)
It's good to give thanks to the Lord! (Ps. 92:1)

Honor your father and mother. (Ex. 20:12)
God gives us rain for seed in the ground. (Is. 30:23)
Love your neighbor as yourself. (Mk. 12:31)
I will sing and praise you, O God! (Ps. 108:1)
God will always love you. (Is. 54:10)
Treat others as you want them to treat you. (Matt. 7:12)
The earth has yielded its fruits; God has blessed us. (Ps. 67:7)
Clap your hands for joy, all peoples!
Praise God with loud songs. (Ps. 67:7)
See what wonderful things God has done! (Ps. 66:5)
You make plants for man to use that he can grow his crops. (Ps. 104:14)
We show love by being kind. (1 Cor. 13:4)
God loves a cheerful giver. (2 Cor. 9:7)
God gives us seed to plant. (2 Cor. 9:10)
With love, help one another. (Gal. 5:13)
Help the needy; spend your money for your brother and friend. (Sir. 29: 9-10)
Do everything with love. (1 Cor. 16:14)
Do good and share what you have. (Heb. 13:16)
Plant gardens and eat what you grow in them. (Jer. 29:5)

AUDIOVISUAL RESOURCES

The following list of resources is recommended for use with three-, four-, and five-year-olds; each resource is marked with the appropriate age. All of these resources have been previewed by the author. However, the importance of preview by the catechist cannot be overemphasized. This advanced review allows the catechist to be familiar with the material before it is presented to the children. It is also good to remember that catechists are able to use these resources in different ways. They are free to stop the sound, interject their own thoughts, use no sound at all, use part of a filmstrip instead of the whole, etc. Be creative!

The filmstrips and videocassettes (noted as VHS) are recommended for three-, four-, and five-year-olds, unless otherwise noted. Names and addresses of producers will be listed at the end.

Church Family and Baptism

1. *Come, Children, Hear Me* (Part 1)
"What Is a Home?" "What Is a Family?"

2. *God's Own Joy* (Episode 3)
"All of Us Together" (5-year-olds only) Discusses aspects of community, beginning with family, friends, community helpers, celebrations and church family.

3. *Marvelous Mystery* (Part 4)
"So Many People" (5-year-olds only) Explains the roles of people who minister during the liturgy. May need some explanation.

Mass

Marvelous Mystery (Part 5)
"So Many Things" (5-year-olds only) Discusses and shows objects used during the liturgy. May need some explanation.

Church Building

Our Church (5-year-olds only) Good filmstrip to be used for a "church tour." Could be used without sound for three- and four-year-olds.

Advent

God Knows My Name
"The Little Fir Tree" The little tree learns to wait and grow and is finally chosen as a family's Christmas tree.

Christmas

1. *Come, Children, Hear Me*
"Jesus Lives" Excellent filmstrip about Jesus for preschool and kindergarten children. Relates the Christmas story, the boyhood of Jesus, and concentrates on the goodness, kindness, and love of the adult Jesus.

2. *Holydays and Holidays*—VHS
"The Ordinary Fir Tree" (5-year-olds only) The story about a tree whose hope to be chosen and decorated for someone's living room is met in an unexpected way.

3. *I Am Special*
"My Friends Are Special" Relates the aspects of friendship through the celebration of a birthday party.

4. *Ronta, the Lucky Donkey*
Short and colorful, tells the Christmas story in a very different and touching manner with a song the children can learn.

5. *The Story Tree Book*
"Spinner's Christmas Gift" Shows that the best gift of all is the gift of yourself.

Valentine's Day

1. *Holydays and Holidays*—VHS
"The Valentine Card" A gift of love can change even the most selfish person.

2. *The Story Tree Book*
"A Beautiful Valentine" A story about a Valentine made and shared with love.

Lent and Saints (Discipleship)

1. *Come, Children, Hear Me*
"Jesus Lives" See Christmas listing.

2. *Holydays and Holidays*—VHS
"Edna the Eagle" "The best way to remember someone is to keep on doing the good things they did."
"Dinty, the Unhappy Leprechaun" A small act of kindness changes Dinty for the better.

Easter

Holydays and Holidays—VHS
"Charles Caterpillar" Charles is "tempted" (to eat corn in the farmer's field) and almost loses his life, but survives and undergoes transformation into a beautiful butterfly.

Pentecost

1. *I Am Special*
"My Friends Are Special" See Christmas listings.

2. *God Is Like: Three Parables for Children* "The Rock," "A Spark of Light," "A Breath of Wind" Use "A Breath of Wind" for this lesson. Good presentation of themes on a concrete level; don't expect the children to apreciate the symbolism or comparison to God.

Thanksgiving

1. *Holydays and Holidays*—VHS
"Billy Beaver"   (5-year-olds only) Shows the value of creation and encourages thankfulness. Includes a surprise ending.

2. *Praise the Lord—Thank You, God*
"Praise the Lord:" Produced without sound, this filmstrip provides pictures for a litany of praise to the Lord for all of creation.
"Thank You, God:" Same as above; use as prayer of thanks for things that surround the children, ie., ice cream cones, balloons, bubble gum, etc., "all the miracles of ordinary living."

3. *The Story Tree Book*
"The Thanksgiving Feast" Presents good ideas about being thankful. Thanksgiving feast is a picnic.

Producers' Addresses

Come, Children, Hear Me
Benziger Publishing Company
15319 Shatsworth Street
Mission Hills, CA 91345
818-898-1391

God Is Like: Three Parables for Children
Alpha Corporation of America
Adapted from the book, *God Is Like*, by Julie Walters and Barbara DeLeu. Published by Ave Maria Press, 1974.

God Knows My Name
Benziger Publishing Company
See *Come, Children, Hear Me.*

God's Joy, Our Joy
Mark IV
Media Resources for Religious Education
2451 East River Road
Dayton, OH 45439
513-294-5785

Holydays and Holidays
Twenty-Third Publications
185 Willow Street
P. O. Box 180
Mystic, CT. 06355
800-321-0411

I Am Special
Our Sunday Visitor
200 Noll Plaza
Huntington, IN 46750
800-348-2440

Ronta, the Lucky Donkey
Twenty-Third Publications
see *Holydays and Holidays*

Marvelous Mystery
Our Sunday Visitor
see *I Am Special*

Our Church
Winston Press
P. O. Box 1630
Hagerstown, MD 21741
800-318-5125

Praise the Lord—Thank You, God
Thomas S. Klise Company
Box 3418
Peoria, IL 61614
309-676-5311

The Story Tree Book
Argus Communications
One DLM Park
Allen, TX 75002
800-527-4747

Notes
for teaching three-, four-, and five-year-old children,
and for celebrating with them.

Notes

for teaching three-, four-, and five-year-old children, and for celebrating with them.

Notes
for teaching three-, four-, and five-year-old children, and for celebrating with them.

Notes

for teaching three-, four-, and five-year-old children, and for celebrating with them.

Notes
for teaching three-, four-, and five-year-old children,
and for celebrating with them.

Notes
for teaching three-, four-, and five-year-old children,
and for celebrating with them.

Notes
for teaching three-, four-, and five-year-old children, and for celebrating with them.